PREPAREDNESS
PEACE

**SIX SESSIONS TO A BASIC FOUNDATION
FOR A LIFESTYLE OF DISASTER PREPAREDNESS**

ENVIRONMENTAL

THUNDERSTORMS

OCE

SUPERCELL

VIOLI

GLOBAL

WELL

SASTER

HURRICANE

TING

ONS

Published by Preparedness Resource Group, LLC.
Preparedness Resource Group, 4300 West Waco Drive, Suite B2-191, Waco, Texas 76710, U.S.A.

Fourth Edition, April 2013

Copyright © Kynada Boland with Scott MacTiernan, 2011
All rights reserved

Boland, Kynada with MacTiernan, Scott. Edited by Raymond, Christine
    Preparedness Peace : Six Sessions to a Basic Foundation for a Lifestyle of Disaster Preparedness / Kynada Boland with Scott MacTiernan.
    Edited by Christine Raymond.

ISBN 978-0615489247
1. Survival skills. 2. Survivalism. 3. Preparedness. 4. Disasters–Social aspects. I Title.

Set in Adobe Garamond
Design by Justin C. Boland

Scripture taken from the HOLY BIBLE, NEW INTERNATIONAL VERSION®. Copyright © 1973, 1978, 1984, 2011 Biblica. Used by permission of Zondervan. All rights reserved. The "NIV" and "New International Version" trademarks are registered in the United States Patent and Trademark Office by Biblica. Use of either trademark requires the permission of Biblica.

Scriptures noted (NASB) are taken from the NEW AMERICAN STANDARD BIBLE®, Copyright © 1960,1962,1963,1968,1971,1972,1973,1975, 1977,1995 by The Lockman Foundation. Used by permission.

CONTENTS

The Preparedness Peace Commitment Card details the accomplishments you will achieve as you complete this six session course. The card is meant to build in personal and team accountability.

Take a moment to really absorb all that needs to be done and will be done in the coming weeks and months. Establishing home and family preparedness has never been so simple or felt so good! Yes, hard work, time, and determination are necessary to accomplish this task, but we know *you can do this!*

PREPAREDNESS PEACE COMMITMENT CARD

I recognize the significance and urgency to prepare my home and family for times of crisis. I commit to attend all six sessions of this course, participate in discussions and accountability, study the Word to understand the Lord's heart in disaster, complete the Preparedness Plans for each session, and accomplish the following basic preparedness:

- *Family Plans and Documents*
  - *Documents copied, distributed, and placed in proper location(s)*
  - *Safe Home Assessment*
  - *Lighting and Energy Plans for power outage*
  - *Evacuation Plans with maps and routes*
  - *Communicate evacuation plans to network*
  - *Intruder De-escalation Plan*
  - *Home Security Plan*

- *Minimum 3 day food storage*
- *Minimum 3 day water storage for family*
- *Car Kit*
- *Home Emergency Supplies*
- *Grab and Go Bags*
- *Shelter-in Place Supplies and room ready*
- *Scripture and devotional studies*

As a symbol of my commitment to doing all that I can to accomplish my basic foundation of preparedness through the structure and tasks set forth in Preparedness Peace, I sign this document and pray for grace, strength, time, and revelation as I pursue preparedness with my family and this team.

Name: _____   Date: _____

The Name is Preparedness Peace!

PRG with film crew

Scott gets Powdered

Welcome to Preparedness Peace. This course is titled Preparedness Peace because as we prepare our homes, families, hearts, and spirits, the Peace of God comes to us. God alone is our true security. He alone sustains us. He is the one who meets every need. We must KNOW Him.

The fact that you are here means that you have embarked on a journey with God, your family, and others to hear what the Lord is saying in this season and to be prepared accordingly. Whether a friend dragged you here or whether there is an urgency in your spirit that you can't quite explain, the Lord will use this course to direct your steps as it relates to preparing your family, home, and spirit.

—Scott & Kelly MacTiernan and Justin & Kynada Boland
Preparedness Resource Group, creators of Preparedness Peace

PUBLISHER'S NOTE

Information presented in this course is collected, organized, and provided for the convenience of the user. However, neither the authors nor the publisher is engaged in rendering professional advice or services to the individual reader. While every effort has been made to keep information accurate and up-to-date, we cannot warrant the authenticity or reliability of such information.

Under no circumstances will the authors nor the publisher be liable for any actions taken, or omissions made, or from reliance on any information contained in, or referenced to, related to this course from any source. Nor shall the authors or the publisher be liable for any other consequences from any such reliance. Further, we will not be liable for any legal claims, damages, or expenses incurred on any decision taken because of using information from the course.

Finally, accordingly nothing in this course is intended as an express or implied warranty of the suitability or fitness of any product, service, or design.

INTRODUCTION

Preparedness Peace is a six-week basic preparedness course designed to build a foundation for a lifestyle of preparedness. This course focuses on Family Plans and Documents, emergency kits and supplies, teamwork, and spiritual preparedness. **As you meet weekly with your group, you will see the value of doing this in the context of a small group – relationship, shared resources and ideas, accountability to complete the homework each week, and the joy of achieving Preparedness Peace.** The Preparedness Plan is made to be relatively simple – though it does require a significant amount of work. **Our definition of basic preparedness is very thorough in scope and means being prepared for a minimum of three days of crisis whether you stay at home or have to evacuate.** Our prayer is that you will take the tools, resources, and progress made during this course and continue on the preparedness journey as far as you desire to go.

COURSE OVERVIEW

All six sessions will follow the same basic structure. Sessions are two hours long, and include a 20-40 minute instructional video with Scott and Kelly MacTiernan. The video segment will focus on unique preparedness topics each session. You will then have an hour to an hour and a half for discussion, questions, team building, Biblical focus, and accountability. In the Preparedness Plan - Take Action section of your workbook, you will find tasks – homework – that will move you step by step toward the goal of accomplishing basic preparedness. It is very important that you do the tasks assigned with each session and not put them off. If you have already achieved basic preparedness, there is still much benefit in taking the course – offering your knowledge and skills to others and continuing to build upon the foundation you have laid.

ARE YOU READY FOR THIS?!

Preparedness Peace is a vehicle to **move** people from knowing they **need** to be prepared to actually **being** prepared. **We want to be very clear that accomplishing the goal of basic preparedness in six structured sessions is meant to be simple, but inevitably will take a significant amount of time, effort, and money. The estimated time requirement is three to five hours each week. The estimated financial commitment can be between $200-$500 based on your personal choices and what you have in your home already. A lack of information is certainly not the cause of unpreparedness, the reason so many are not yet prepared is because of the work required to achieve it.** Rest assured, you will **never** regret the time and energy spent preparing your home and family for crisis. Preparedness Peace will build an excellent foundation for three weeks, months, and years of preparedness and you will be ready to serve as the Lord will lead.

We know there are volumes and volumes of preparedness information and resources available online and at conferences and seminars. We will reference these resources and encourage you to use them because many are excellent and informative. The strength of Preparedness Peace is found in helping you to **accomplish** preparedness in community.

PARTICIPANT WORKBOOK CONTENTS

As part of your Preparedness Peace Participant Workbook you received:

- Preparedness Supply Lists
  - Prep Step Inventory
  - Grab and Go Bag
  - Home Emergency Supplies
  - Car Kit, Personal Awareness Quiz
  - Three Weeks to Three Month Supplies
- Emergency Family Plans and Document templates

We recommend obtaining a 3-ring binder with dividers to store hard copies of the emergency family plans and other documents that will make up your personal preparedness library. There are instructions for the binder in the Lists section of workbook. The Participant Workbook and the forms, plans and documents provided in it are meant to be the beginning of your library, but as you find websites, discover articles, and other resources that you like, add them to the binder. Make your hard copies now. If you are relying on an electronic version of everything you find helpful regarding preparedness, you may end up disappointed in the event that there is no power when you need the information most.

The workbook is an important resource as well. It contains a summary of all the video teachings, video and discussion questions, tools and helpful lists. An additional section is the, Are you Ready for This?! challenges for those who want to dive deeper into preparedness. Lastly, of utmost importance, are the daily devotionals. This is an opportunity to dig into the Word and seek the Lord about who He is in crisis, how He is leading you to prepare and to hear His promises over your life. True peace and security come from the Lord. We really hope this workbook will serve as a resource for years to come. This is not just about homework, building a pack, and getting food on the shelf. We are trying to help you develop the mind-set of a preparedness lifestyle. Take the time now, build it in to your schedule, and enjoy preparedness peace.

It is important to note, that this course has been designed so that anyone who has *taken* the course and has accomplished basic preparedness may lead the course for others. You do not have to be a preparation expert, you just need to be convinced of the value of preparedness and the Lord's plans to use you in times of crisis. Our hope is that you will take this to your neighborhoods, work places, and social circles to build relationship, share the love of Jesus, and get your city prepared.

We commend you for making the commitment to establish your family's Preparedness Peace.

As you begin today, we pray the Lord will speak to you about your personal preparation, people to team up with, give you strategy for your neighborhood, and revelation about who He is in the midst of crisis.

Hebrews 10:23-25 "*Let us hold unswervingly to the hope we profess, for he who promised is faithful. And let us consider how we may spur one another on toward love and good deeds. Let us not give up meeting together as some are in the habit of doing, but let us encourage one another all the more as you see the Day approaching.*"

ABOUT THE
AUTHORS

JUSTIN & KYNADA BOLAND

The Boland's story is unique in that they met and married in the context of the Haiti earthquake in 2010. They both served in the capacity of On the Ground Director for different relief organizations operating in Port au Prince. Justin and Kynada have seen crisis reveal the need for encounter with God and are passionate about equipping people to respond from that place.

Kynada has a rich teaching history in the urban classroom and in the wilderness. She spent four years with Crisis Response International as Director of Training and as visionary and author of Preparedness Peace, she is excited about establishing families in a foundation of preparedness.

Justin is the creative visionary, problem solving, graphic designer behind Preparedness Peace curriculum and by profession. He is passionate about the Church and the opportunity to come together in crisis, share the love of Jesus, and minister His heart and words to those who are hurting.

Justin and Kynada call Houston, Texas their home and work with Somebody Cares International. Their primary focus is Global Compassion Response Network.

SCOTT & KELLY MACTIERNAN

Scott & Kelly MacTiernan spent 30 years owning and operating a Dude and Guest Ranch in the southwest mountains of Colorado. Scott was also a ski instructor, EMT, and Hunting Guide and Outfitter during much of that time. Their skills and experience have equipped them in a lifestyle of preparedness.

Their involvement and training from ministries that respond to crisis both nationally and internationally has also equipped them. Their love for survival skills and the prudence of preparedness has developed into a training that they are passionate about sharing. They love teaching and leading others and seeing individuals and families become more equipped to endure possible crisis.

They joyfully reside in Kansas City, MO near their four grown children and granddaughters and currently serve as community intercessors and Prayer Room Staff at the International House of Prayer.

WHY ME?
WHY PREPARE?
SESSION ONE

VIEWER GUIDE

NOTES

_____

_____

_____

_____

_____

_____

_____

_____

_____

_____

_____

_____

_____

_____

_____

_____

WHY ME?
WHY PREPARE?

1.) Many people do not prepare because they think disaster will not _____ to them or because thinking about preparing for disaster stirs up fear.

2.) Preparation can eliminate _____.

3.) We want you to finish this course with _____ knowing you *are* prepared and that you have good reason to be prepared.

4.) This basic foundation of preparedness is meant to establish you in a _____ of preparedness.

5.) The benefits of having a _____ are accountability, security, resources, etc.

6.) Our current lifestyle of _____ makes it difficult to imagine not having quick solutions to all needs.

7.) By now you should feel an _____ to prepare.

*T*he fact that you are here states that you know you need to be prepared or that, at least, someone has convinced you to get prepared. Or maybe you have so much experience and knowledge on this topic that you should be telling **us** why it's time to get prepared. Either way, it is prudent and brilliant to have your home and family prepared for any personal crises that may occur as well as the large-scale, regional, and national disasters we see on the rise.

Most people have experienced personal crisis – a power outage, car wreck, a health emergency, flooding, ice storms, or fire – at some time in their life. Have you? Were you prepared? Do you wish that you had been more prepared? Are there ways that you can now see that forethought and planning could have eased the situation?

There are those of you that have been involved in larger scale disasters – hurricanes, tornadoes, earthquakes, or forced evacuation of some sort. Anyone with personal or secondary experience has certainly gleaned insights in the process. There are benefits in every disaster scenario for having a plan that your whole family knows about and has practiced. ***There is a peace that comes in being prepared.***

Furthermore, natural disasters are ripping through cities and nations. "In the U.S., there were more tornadoes in April 2011 than in any month in history." (Rice) Seismologists predict major American fault lines to shake in the near future. "The fact is most states are at risk of major earthquakes, with 39 of the 50 states in moderate to high risk areas for seismic activity." (Kanalley)

The economics of the world look shaky as well – including Japan, the Middle East, Europe, and the United States. In the United States specifically, consider the current unemployment rate, inflation, housing crashes, and the recent increase in gas and food prices.

So why is it that our grandparents were better prepared than we are?

It is not common practice to have much – if anything – stored away for a rainy day. Why would we store it when we can go to the store and pick up whatever we need? In our defense, preparation skills – gardening, canning, farming, storing, and planning – are not something that most of us grew up with or have learned from our families (with the exception of a few). However, the complex supply system we rely on is only several hours deep. This system is only able to supply if all elements of transport, communication, and availability are in place, manned, and working. If you pull out one of these components then the fragility of our system is clearly revealed.

In the event of a city or statewide disaster, history proves that grocery store shelves can empty in as few as 24 hours. Water for purchase is certainly a limited supply and gas stations would have lines circling the block and eventually run out – given they had the power to pump it.

Our culture has created this thin veneer of safety, stability, and security.

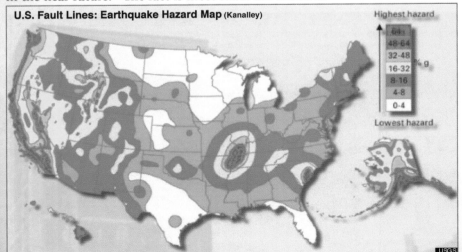

U.S. Fault Lines: Earthquake Hazard Map (Kanalley)

Highest hazard

64+
48-64
32-48
16-32
8-16
4-8
0-4

%g

Lowest hazard

USGS

Many populated areas in the U.S. have a high probability of earthquakes.

As more U.S. currency is put into circulation the value of the dollar declines.

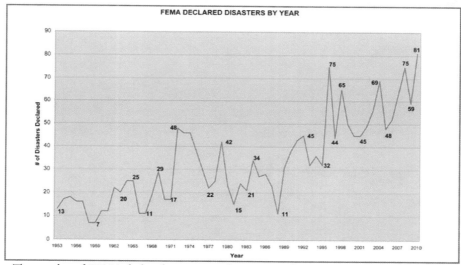

The number of FEMA declared emergencies has continued to increase over the past 50 years.

In our culture we are used to convenience and immediate gratification. One could find almost anything they need with a click of the button, a roll up to the drive-thru, or one of many other methods invented to give you what you want when you want it. Even in Scripture, some people thought they could buy oil at the last minute when they needed it (Matthew 25:1-13). This – as we see in the parable of the ten virgins – is not always true and it is not true for us today – both in the physical realm and in the spiritual realm.

Preparing *now* **– storing necessary items, making detailed plans, pursuing Jesus daily – is the** *key* **to Preparedness Peace.**

You and your family will have a foundation of security and confidence that you can stand on and move forward with in times of crisis. As you progress on the preparedness journey, you will learn that there are many more people preparing today than you would have ever thought. Enjoy walking this out with other like-minded people pursuing preparedness and pursuing Jesus. Preparedness Peace is meant to give you tools, resources, and accountability so that you can build a foundation of preparedness that will allow you to care for your family, serve others, and partner with the Lord in any way that He leads. We desire that through this course you will develop a lifestyle of preparedness both physically and spiritually.

The small group that you are working with during this course IS your team. You don't have to be best friends, but you do need to learn to work together, and acknowledge each other's gifts and the things that each person brings to the team. There are many facets of preparedness and people are created uniquely to serve the body in specific ways (1 Corinthians 12). Dig for the treasures in your teammates and call them forth, hold each other accountable to the task you have committed to so that you may work and grow together during this course.

* Recommended discussion questions

1.)* Why are you here? What is motivating you to this preparedness lifestyle?

_____
_____
_____

2.)* Based on what you know about the course and its requirements so far, what are your first questions, thoughts, concerns, ideas?

_____
_____

3.) On a scale of 1 to 10, (1 being the lowest, you have canned foods in pantry, 10 being self-sustained for three months) how prepared are you right now?

1 – 2 – 3 – 4 – 5 – 6 – 7 – 8 – 9 – 10

Prepared for _____ days and for _____ people.

4.) What personal skills do you bring to the team that offer strength in preparedness and crisis? Medical, canning, home schooling, administration, military experience, camping, hunting, intercession and security are just a few of the many valuable attributes for preparedness.

_____
_____

5.) What are your three biggest fears about disaster or times of crisis? While this course encompasses basic preparedness, we need to consider preparedness for greater disasters such as famine, civil unrest, separation during crisis, and long-term emergencies. Does fear creep in when you consider a shortage of water? Starvation? Death? Violence?

_____
_____

6.)* What is your favorite thing about God and why? *[For example, Kynada's favorite thing about God is His faithfulness. Regardless of my full faith or lack of faithfulness in different seasons of life, and also through really hard seasons – miscarriage, dad's death – the Lord has revealed Himself as so faithful. I trust Him to show up. This is one of the things I love about God.]*

_____
_____
_____

7.) What is your perspective of God in times of personal crisis, localized crisis, or national crisis? How do you **feel** about Him when hard times happen to you and to others?

_____

_____

_____

 ## Biblical Focus and Discussion

Preview and discuss the verses to be studied during the week. Read each scripture aloud as a group and discuss first impressions, any current or past revelation on that verse, and pray together that God would speak to you as you study His Scripture this week.

SESSION ONE | DAY ONE

**Matthew 7:24-25** "Therefore everyone who hears these words of mine and puts them into practice is like a wise man who built his house on the rock. The rain came down, the streams rose, and the winds blew and beat against that house; yet it did not fall, because it had its foundation on the rock."

SESSION ONE | DAY TWO

**Matthew 6:33** "But seek first his kingdom and his righteousness, and all these things will be given to you as well."

SESSION ONE | DAY THREE

**Matthew 6:25** "Therefore I tell you, do not worry about your life, what you will eat or drink; or about your body, what you will wear. Is not life more important than food, and the body more important than clothes?"

SESSION ONE | DAY FOUR

**Genesis 6:9, 13-15** "...Noah was a righteous man, blameless among the people of his time, and he walked with God. So God said to Noah, "I am going to put an end to all people, for the earth is filled with violence because of them. I am surely going to destroy both them and the earth. So make yourself an ark of cypress wood; make rooms in it and coat it with pitch inside and out. This is how you are to build it..."

SESSION ONE | DAY FIVE

Prayer Focus: _____

Praying for someone or something is the most effective way to gain God's heart for that person or situation. Spend this time praying for the situation your class has decided upon. Ask God to speak to you about specific people or details in this situation. What moves your heart as you pray? Do you find yourself praying in a more specific direction? Stick with this and ask the Lord to reveal MORE to you today. Share with your group what God is highlighting to you about this topic in your prayer time.

1.) Choose an accountability partner or couple from within your small group. Call them once during each week of the course to check on progress. **Stop and choose your buddy now.**

Name:_____ Phone #_____ Email _____

2.) Make time in your schedule – three to five hours – each week to accomplish the homework assigned for each session. (It **will** require **this** much time to accomplish the tasks for each session). Write the days and times that you will designate for these tasks.

Monday: _____   Thursday: _____
Tuesday: _____   Friday: _____
Wednesday: _____   Saturday: _____

3.) Using the Prep Step Inventory List provided – which includes all items from the Home Emergency Supplies, Car Kit, and Grab and Go Bag lists – **inventory** what you **have** already in your home and identify what you will need to do, purchase, and procure in the coming weeks. Bring the inventory results with you to the next session.

_____   _____   _____
_____   _____   _____

4.) Find two examples of record breaking disasters in the last year and write them here: _____   _____

5.) Complete the Personal Awareness Quiz handout located in the Lists section. If it is too much for one session, spread the questions between sessions. Always bring your completed responses to class the next session.

❏ I have completed the Personal Awareness Quiz.

6.) Accept your invitation to the Prepare to Share Facebook page, read some articles that interest you, and make an introduction post.

❏ I made a post on Prepare to Share   ❏ I am not on Facebook

7.) Read and respond to this session's daily devotionals on the following pages.

YouTube: History Channel, After Armageddon, Sessions 1-2
Resources: www.americanpreppersnetwork.blogspot.com
Websites: www.Bolands.ThriveLife.com
Scripture: Matthew 25:1-13; John 10:27-30

The Wisdom of Hearing and Obeying the Lord
Read Matthew 7:24-27; Psalm 25:12

The first passage makes it clear that our protection is directly related to listening and obeying the Lord's instructions. We see that the rains (troubles, disaster) came against both the house of the wise man and the foolish man. The lesson of the foolish man is that there are negative consequences for the man (or woman) who hears the words of the Lord and does not put them into practice.

1.) Both the wise and foolish man heard the words of the Lord, but only one chose to obey. Do you agree that your protection is directly related to listening and obeying the Lord's instructions? How do you put that into practice in your everyday life? Ask the Lord to clearly speak to you during this course and make a commitment to obey Him when He speaks to you.

_____

_____

2.) Do you recognize there are negative consequences for individuals who decide not to obey the Lord? Reflect on situations in your past where you did not obey the Lord. Were you able to see the consequences? How will you use that information in light of your Preparedness Peace (and life) journey?

_____

_____

3.) We know that the storms of life **are** coming and our choice in preparing for them and in the midst of them is whether we choose to trust the voice of the Lord. Scripture is clear, God speaks to us, His children. Do you believe you can hear His voice in these important areas of your life? What are some ways in your past where the Lord has proven His faithfulness and trustworthiness to you?

_____

_____

4.) Psalm 25:12 is an incredible promise for those who fear Him! The Lord has promised to instruct us about decisions for our lives. We encourage you to have faith in His promise and to ask Him to instruct you each day about specific decisions you need to make in your preparedness journey.

_____

_____

_____

Seek First the Kingdom of God
Read Matthew 6:25-34

This is **so much** more than a passage commanding us not to worry about our own personal needs, although that is true. It is full of **hope** for each one of us, for the Lord tells us that He already knows what we need. The Lord also tells us how willing He is to provide us with all that we need, as we are of such great value to Him. The **key** to the whole passage is found in this quote: "But seek first his kingdom and his righteousness, and all these things will be given to you as well." All these things refer to **all** of your preparedness needs for not only three days, but your entire life. The goal in preparedness and in every other area of your life must be to seek the Lord, allow Him to speak to you about each area of your life and then obey what He has to say and trust Him to do the rest. That will bring you true Preparedness Peace. The truth is that the Lord is the only One who knows what will be coming on the earth, even to your neighborhood, and what you need to be prepared for. Not only that, He has promised if you put Him first and seek Him, He will show you what you need and provide it for you.

1.) The KEY to the whole passage is found in this quote: "But seek first his kingdom and his righteousness, and all these things will be given to you as well." In what areas of your life do you currently seek the Lord? In what areas of your life could you be seeking Him more? Are there areas in your life that you find you do not seek the Lord about?

_____

_____

_____

2.) Set your heart to obey this passage and to truly "...seek first his kingdom and his righteousness..." What would this look like in your daily life?

_____

_____

_____

3.) We know that all we need in the area of preparedness will be provided as we seek Him first. Ask Him what that looks like in crisis. Lord, how do I seek you first in crisis?

_____

_____

_____

Do Not Worry
Read Matthew 6:25-34

1.) Most of us have worried about our personal needs in the past in one area or another. What are the areas that most concern you in your life now? Are there areas in your life that you have not surrendered your worry over to the Lord? Talk to the Lord about these areas and ask Him for insight on how to trust Him to provide all that you need.

2.) In verses 26 and 28 it literally says "look" at the birds of the air and "see" how the lilies grow. Go outside or position yourself in a place where you can actively observe nature. Record seven observations or insights you gain from this time.

_____

_____

_____

3.) Do you truly understand how much the Lord values you? Not for what you do, but for who you are. Think about the examples used in this passage: birds, flowers, and grass. Reflect on your time observing God in nature. Do you believe that the Lord values you more than these things? Reflect on your value to the Lord – ask the Holy Spirit to speak to you and reveal to you how much the Lord values you.

_____

_____

_____

— Session One —
Day Four Devotional

Noah is Prepared through the Lord's Instruction
Read Genesis 6:9, 13-22

I love this picture of the heart of the Lord. He cares enough to not only tell Noah about the disaster coming on the earth, but provided Noah with detailed instructions about how he could save himself and his family long before the disaster struck. In this hour the Lord desires to do the same with us – Lord, give us ears to hear and a heart to obey. My favorite part of this passage is the very end where it says "Noah did everything just as God commanded him." My desire is that the Lord would be able to say the same for me and you! As you can see from this passage, the Lord did not leave it to chance, but instead gave Noah very specific instructions about how to build the ark.

As you go through this course and fill your pantry, your grab and go bag, and car kit with supplies, *know* that the Lord will guide you so that you will have all that you need when the time comes. **The Lord gave specific instructions about how to build his shelter, what animals to bring with him and also specified that Noah was "...to take every kind of food that is to be eaten and store**

it away as food for you and for them [the animals]." The Lord cares about the details of our preparation. Noah believed God and built a *boat* when it had not yet *ever* rained on the earth before. We can see the troubles and disaster on the Earth – it requires much less faith from us to believe we need to prepare. **The *key* to being prepared is to *listen* for the Lord's voice and then heed what you hear.**

1.) Think about your relationship with the Lord and how you would respond if He asked you to do something like He asked Noah to do. One present-day example might be to move to a far away place that you have never been to. What would you do? How easy or difficult would it be to obey Him? How about if the Lord spoke to you about ways that you need to be prepared that you were not planning?

_____

_____

_____

2.) The beginning of this passage makes it clear that Noah was one who "...walked with God." Verse 13 begins with "So God said to Noah..." and He shares with Noah what He is about to do on the earth. There seems to be a direct correlation between Noah's walk with the Lord and what the Lord reveals to him. Reflect on this and ask the Lord to reveal more to you about what He is doing on the Earth – or in your city – and specifically how to achieve basic preparedness in the next six sessions.

_____

_____

_____

3.) Hearing and obeying the Lord throughout our preparedness journey gives us confidence about our preparations. The Lord gave instructions to Noah to make provision not only for him, but for his family to be protected in the midst of the destruction of the whole earth. Who does the Lord want you to make provision for – in the short-term and in the long-term? Ask the Lord with whom He would have you to share Preparedness Peace. Consider leading a future small group for your family, your church, or your neighbors.

_____

_____

_____

—— Session One ——
Day Five Prayer Topic

Pray for _____

*Spend this time praying for the situation your class has decided upon. Ask God to speak to you about specific people or details in this situation. What moves your heart as you pray? Do you find yourself praying in a more specific direction? Stick with this and ask the Lord to reveal **more** to you today.*

_____

_____

_____

_____

TEAMWORK &
POWER OF A PLAN
SESSION TWO

NOTES

_____

_____

_____

_____

_____

_____

_____

_____

_____

_____

_____

_____

_____

_____

TEAMWORK & POWER OF A PLAN

1.) _____ is key to being truly prepared.

2.) Two disadvantages of "going solo" in preparedness are limited _____ and _____.

3.) Although you are part of a team you are individually _____ to be prepared on your own.

4.) A failure to plan is a plan to _____.

5.) A plan brings _____, direction, and purpose, key elements missing in disaster.

Relationship is key to being truly prepared. Unless you plan on going solo every element of preparedness will involve planning and working together with other people. The Lord loves relationship. Even He operates within the Trinity. He established the **body of Christ** to function together with its strengths – and weaknesses – to reveal the nature and beauty and power of God (1 Cor 12:12-27). Throughout this course there will be opportunity to develop relationship with the Lord, your family, your small group, and ultimately with your neighborhood or anyone you invite to pursue preparedness with you.

What makes a *team* so valuable are the unique gifts, skills, experiences, and heart that each individual contributes to make up the whole. The foundation of teamwork must be built on mutual edification and calling forth of the gifts and strengths of every team member – even children and the elderly. *every* person has something valuable to add to the whole.

There are many advantages of pursuing preparedness as a team. Whether your team is your family unit or extends to several households in your neighborhood, when working together you can create a plan and implement it. Sharing resources makes the whole greater than that of any individual. Because of the varied strengths and skills of yourself and others on your team, you will be able to better steward all that you have collectively. Tough decisions may be weighed and made in the safety of a team. A strong team structure covers areas of weakness and allows the team to thrive. The team element also provides ongoing accountability to **get prepared** and follow through with plans when necessary. Mind you, working as a team does not negate your individual responsibility to prepare. What makes a strong team is each member offering their best to the whole. Community is the only answer for resources, support,

strength, safety, and recovery during times of crisis.

This idea of operating as a team can be difficult for us today because we are mobile, social, independent, and, quite honestly, we tend to carry a entitlement attitude. Living in true community is difficult, requires a lot of give and take, and you will have to give up the comforts and luxuries you may be used to. In the time of crisis we will have to give up things that we believe are our rights. This is where *loving* people really comes into play.

We asked you to choose a buddy so that you will see the value of working together in preparedness. Buddy may be a childish term, but it represents a significant role in preparedness. As you serve your buddy by holding them accountable to the goals they have set, pray for them and check in with them along this journey. **We are certain you will see what a blessing it is to do this alongside other like-minded people.**

Planning is another key element of preparedness. Benjamin Franklin (they think) once said, "Failure to plan is a plan to fail." We will not fail. In Christ, we are *more* than conquerors (Romans 8:37) and we are taking these six weeks of our life to make a plan and to *be prepared*.

This is where the labor intensive work happens. Many people enjoy planning fishing trips, family vacations, etc. This is good and those planning skills will help you here. However, doing this well is *much* more work and the fruit of your labors may not be realized for weeks or even years. Yet we know the value of these plans far exceed that of any vacation. **You must be deliberate about accomplishing all that must be done with the Family Plans and Documents.**

It is important that you grasp how critical this documentation will be to your family in a time of crisis. Here is a personal story from Kynada to illustrate this point. In 2004 I was in the southern islands of Thailand, standing on a 12 foot sea wall watching the tsunami suck the water out to sea and then with all its force, hurl it back up onto the shore. By divine protection, our private taxi pulled up just at this moment and drove us away from the shore. Immediately the Lord spoke two passages into my heart: Isaiah 55 and Isaiah 43. In Isaiah 43 it says, "But now, this is what the Lord says, He who created you, He who formed you. Fear not, for I have redeemed you, I have summoned you by name, you are mine..." I prayed this passage over us as we continued to drive. Minutes later, our taxi driver informed us that he heard on the radio our original destination – Phuket airport – was underwater. Needless to say, this was a very intense time for us! Many conversations, prayers, and hours later we got into another taxi and our driver drove us all the way to Bangkok – a 12 hour drive.

By the time we arrived in Bangkok, it was mid-morning on Christmas Day in America. News of the tsunami was streaming on every channel. My parents, brother, and grandparents *all* saw the news. Because my parents had

requested that I give them our detailed itinerary, contact information, and copies of our passports for everyone on the trip, my parents knew right where we were – exactly where the tsunami had hit – and my dad activated all his plans right away. He contacted the US Embassy in Bangkok and faxed our itinerary and passport photos to every facet of government stated to be working towards recovery and relief. Because he had our itineraries, he was able to do all he could possibly do and then wait, pray, and watch with the rest of my family. While this was still a *very* intense time for everyone involved, he had a measure of peace knowing that he had done everything he could.

In Thailand we were unable to read the red and orange letters flashing on the screen, so we resorted to playing cards on the airport floor until we got a tearful, desperate call from my friends' family in the States and then another call. With each call our understanding of the proportions of the disaster broadened. I called my mom to tell her I was okay and her response was sobs of relief and thankfulness to the Lord.

The documentation and details that you will prepare during this course *will* give you peace in the event that you really need to use them. This documentation will help you to claim your children in a shelter situation, the photos will help identify people who are close to you, and knowing evacuation plans and routes will help you find people when communication is down. Knowing that these plans are in place lends security to those hoping to be found and the ones seeking them.

The objective of all this planning is to *thrive* in the midst of crisis and be able to reveal the love of Christ to others. In Genesis 41, Joseph was positioned by God to help prepare a nation for seven years of famine. The Lord gave him a specific strategy and the favor of the king to carry it out. A good plan brings comfort, direction, and purpose – elements missing in disaster. In the workbook you will find all the necessary Family Plans and Documents, including detailed lists of documents to copy, emergency contact information to keep and to share, evacuation plans, Memorandums of Understanding (MOUs), and emergency lists. Please do not put off this work. It will require a significant amount of time and energy, but it will be *so* worth it. More detailed information regarding evacuation plans may be found in Session 5.

Communication: We didn't mention this as a specific item for the Family Plans, but it is something that deserves great consideration and planning. In a disaster situation communication lines are typically either overwhelmed or down in the first phase of the crisis. Your family will need to have ways to get current information. A shortwave radio will allow you to hear local news around the world. You also will want a way to communicate with one another outside of telephone, email, etc. Oftentimes sending a text message will still work, but there is also a chance it won't. When the big disaster comes HAM radios will be a real asset. You must be licensed to operate a HAM radio. Look into training and testing at www.arrl.org, The National Association for Amateur Radio. The main point is to develop what you have; don't wait until the day you need it to try and get communication plans in place.

HAM RADIO INFORMATION

Take the Amateur Radio Technician license test and purchase an amateur HAM radio. To study, purchase the ARRL Ham Radio License Manual or study online with www.hamtestonline.com, the highest rated online prep course. Http://hamexam.org/ has all current exams posted, tracks your progress, and gives questions based on in/correct answers.

Two recommended beginner radios are Yaesu FT-60 handheld or FT-8800. More advanced radios; Yaesu FT-897. (really 3 radios in one), Yaesu FT-857 (same but smaller) or Yaesu FT-8800. Places to buy radios: gigaparts.com, hamradio.com, aesham.com: All you need is the radio, battery, and antennae.

Shortwave radios are able to tune into local and international news. We recommend the Eton FR600 Shortwave and All Alert radio. It accomplishes many of the points covered previously and the following, such as Emergency Light, Power, Shortwave, plus All Alert Radio with NOAA, Amber, and other local hazard/emergency alerts. Don't forget extra batteries.

Communication is especially important for a good security plan. When phone service is available, pre-planned, brief texts are a quiet and fairly effective way to communicate. Hand-held radios work well, flashlights, and laser pointers can also be used for security communication purposes if you have practiced and others can understand what you are communicating.

CASH

Another thing you will really need to think about as you plan for crisis is **cash**! In the event of power outages, stores can and do stop giving change, accepting checks, or running credit cards. Additionally, banks and ATMs may be closed, so having cash on hand is a must. Keep at least $100-$250 per person, more if you can afford it. No bills should be larger than $20s. Have some coins available also. Hide these funds in an unusual place that is not easily accessible. (Don't put it in the freezer or toilet tank – every thief checks those places.)

DOCUMENTATION

As you begin to make these plans and gather documentation, you will come to some hard questions. Don't shy away from them, jot them down, talk about them, and most importantly, pray about them. Questions like: "If we evacuate, how will we bring grandma with us? Will she want to go? Is she physically able to go? What if you are walking? What if someone you think will evacuate with you refuses to go? What about pets?" Take some time to consider your unique situation to determine what your specific preparedness needs may be. By making special considerations and plans in advance, you are loving others well. These questions left unanswered will make you part of the disaster... so think about them in advance and be ready. Additional hard questions might be the ones you get asked. As you distribute the necessary documents to family and friends, they will have questions as well. Think about how other people will respond to your interest in preparedness. Another plan to have in place is how to take this opportunity to share the love of Jesus, the *good* plans that He has for us, and how He is the One who gives the peace that cannot be taken away. Ever. Are you ready for this?!

These plans and documentation are a critical element of your preparedness foundation. Like other areas of preparedness, your plans will need to be revisited, reviewed, and kept up-to-date, but you should take great delight in this accomplishment. This is huge.

Disabilities and Special Needs

Creating a disaster preparedness plan that includes people with disabilities or special needs is not as complicated as you might think. If you carefully think out the answers to the questions below, you'll help people with special needs successfully navigate an emergency.

Who will be responsible for assisting the person with special needs? When a disaster strikes, you'll have a lot of responsibility as the plan leader. If possible, designate someone else to be in charge of caring for, assisting and monitoring the person with special needs in your group.

What mobility needs do you need to consider? Is there any chance you'll have to evacuate to a shelter, another city or even out-of-state? You need to consider this possibility when you're making your emergency preparations. Plan for the mobility needs of the special needs person you're caring for. Is your primary vehicle the right choice to transport everyone—including the person with special needs—should you have to leave home?

Will transportation assistance be needed to evacuate in advance of a hurricane? In a number of states, there is a special assistance registry for people who are unable to evacuate on their own. Dial 2-1-1 to find out if your state has this service. To arrange for transportation for yourself or a family member, call 2-1-1. **It's important to remember that 2-1-1 is not an emergency number** **2·1·1** **to call during a storm – you must pre-register for evacuation transportation.**

Does a plan member have special medication needs? People with special needs may require routine medications as part of their daily treatment. Do you have a complete list of medications, dosages and times they should be taken? Do you have copies of prescriptions to show emergency/rescue personnel? Is there someone in your family or group who will monitor a dosage schedule and administer medications?

Are you prepared for a prolonged stay away from home? In a serious emergency, you might find your time away from home extended by weeks or even months, so you have to consider how you'll handle a prolonged evacuation period for a person with special needs. Where will you go? Are you aware of medical professionals in the area who can provide the special services required? Do you know where you'll fill prescriptions or restock the special supplies you might need? If you need dialysis treatments, do you know where facilities are located?

Pets

For many people, their pets are like members of the family. Yet, too often, family pets are overlooked during disaster planning. Here's what you need to consider to protect your pets during a disaster.

How many pets do you need to plan for? Some families have more than one pet; others have an assortment of animals. When you're making your emergency preparations, you'll need to take into account the type of pet(s) you're planning for. How big are they? Do your pets get along with one another?

Are there any special needs you need to consider for your pet(s)? Just like their owners, pets have special needs that must be addressed when you create your preparedness plan. Do they need any special medications or foods?

How will you transport your pet(s)? Emergency situations often require families to leave home and relocate to shelters, other cities, or even out of state. Your disaster preparedness plans need to include how you will move your animals with your family. Do you have enough cages to contain your pets comfortably? Do you have enough food and water in your travel supplies? Is there enough room in your vehicle for your family, your pets, their cages and your supplies?

Have you completed your pre-planning for your pet preparations? Making an emergency plan that includes your pet's needs means doing a little homework ahead of time. Before you can commit to a plan, you have to make sure all the pieces are in place. Do you have a list of hotels/motels that accept pets? Do you have proof that you registered and vaccinated your pet in case you need to go to a shelter?

This information provided by Texas Department of State Health Services ©2007.

33

Choose three or more of the questions below and share the answers in your group now.
* Recommended discussion questions

1.) What are some advantages and disadvantages to going solo? Do you feel like you want to go solo? Why or why not?

_____

_____

2.) What do you see as advantages to building preparedness around a team? What are the things that become more difficult working as a team?

_____

_____

3.)* Do you **like** working with a team? Do you have personal experience working together with others? (This preparedness team will be very diverse – made up of people of different ages, skill sets, interests, and experiences – which will add both depth to your team and an element of challenge to the team.)

_____

_____

4.) The Family Plans and Documents that must be prepared can be daunting. Share with the group your strategy for accomplishing large projects like this.

_____

_____

5.)* What are the tough questions you will have to answer when creating Family Plans, which could determine your decision to stay or evacuate? Pets? Parents in a nursing home? Medical situations? Security?

_____

_____

6.) How do you think others – especially those closest to you – will respond to your interest in preparedness? Could their response derail your motivation and progress towards preparedness? You must be committed to accomplish the task otherwise naysayers may have more influence on you than you wish.

_____

_____

7.)* Discuss your results from the Personal Awareness Quiz. Were there any surprising findings? Were you able to identify your personal strengths?

_____

_____

Biblical Focus and Discussion

Preview and discuss the verses to be studied during the week. Read each scripture aloud as a group and discuss first impressions, any current or past revelation on that verse, and pray together that God would speak to you as you study His Scripture this week.

SESSION TWO | DAY ONE

Hebrews 10:23-25 "Let us hold unswervingly to the hope we profess, for he who promised is faithful. And let us consider how we may spur one another on toward love and good deeds. Let us not give up meeting together as some are in the habit of doing, but let us encourage one another all the more as you see the Day approaching."

SESSION TWO | DAY TWO

Genesis 41:25b "God has revealed to Pharaoh what he is about to do."
Genesis 41:32 "The reason the dream was given to Pharaoh in two forms is that the matter has been firmly decided by God, and God will do it soon."

SESSION TWO | DAY THREE

Genesis 41:39-40 "Then Pharaoh said to Joseph, 'Since God has made all this known to you, there is no one so discerning and wise as you. You shall be in charge of my palace, and all my people are to submit to your orders. Only with respect to the throne will I be greater than you.'"

SESSION TWO | DAY FOUR

Proverbs 27:12 "The prudent see danger and take refuge, but the simple keep going and suffer for it."

SESSION TWO | DAY FIVE

Prayer Focus: _____

YouTube: History Channel, After Armageddon, Sessions 3-4
Website: www.americansnetworkingtosurvive.org
Online Planning Resource: http://ready.adcouncil.org/fep/
Scripture: Matthew 24:36-51; 1 Corinthians 12:12-27
Book: *When All Plans Fail* by MD Paul R. Williams

This week you will begin the process of preparing Family Plans and Documents – which includes written plans and procuring the necessary documentation that you will copy to keep in a safe box and in your grab and go bag (not to mention making copies for other members of your family so that they have them too). We have split the tasks up between the next several sessions for easier management of this significant task. If you wish to do it all this week, **GO FOR IT!** If you wish to spread it out, follow the Family Plans and Documents tasks divided up on task #4 in Sessions 3, 4, and 5. You will have all documents and plans complete by Session 6.

1.) Start thinking about the people you would want to pursue preparedness and planning with. Maybe it is your family alone or you and your best friends or the family next door. Either way, think about it and begin to dream about how it could go.

Write the names of the people that you would want on your future preparedness team here:
_____, _____, _____, _____, _____,
_____, _____, _____, _____, _____.

2.) Gather and prepare *all* personal documents (see Comprehensive List of Suggested Documents to Copy on the following page). In future sessions, you will make *copies* for the grab and go bags, for each child (when appropriate), and an additional copy to be placed in a firebox and/or water proof bag. Check the documents you plan to copy. Keep track of your progress on the next page.

3.) Identify primary locations where your family is daily and begin to think about evacuation plans from home, school, and work to a chosen destination. Consider as many details as possible, including primary and alternative routes.

Primary Locations	Evacuation Destinations
_____	_____
_____	_____
_____	_____
_____	_____

4.) Make a list of all the things you use water for in your personal life. Approximately how many gallons of water do you think you use each day?
_____
_____
_____
_____

5.) Find two preparedness resource websites that you like or found helpful. Write websites here and post them on Prepare-to-Share. Next session, share these resources with your class.
_____   _____

6.) Read and respond to this session's daily devotionals on the following pages.

Comprehensive List of Suggested Documents to Copy

Yes the list is daunting; only copy what applies to you or is relevant to your needs. It is also your personal discretion which documents you choose to place in Grab and Go Bags, and share with others; i.e. adult children, relatives, etc. Do be sure to put the originals in a fire safe box.

ADDRESSES:
- ❏ ICE-In case of Emergency contacts
- ❏ Name, Address, Phone #, Emails of Family, Friends, Business, Christmas card list Etc.

AUTOMOBILE & VEHICLES:
- ❏ Auto Policy, Insurance card on each car
- ❏ Auto Loan documents
- ❏ Title/or leases
- ❏ RV/Boat Titles/loans
- ❏ Warranty, Record of Repairs

CHURCH:
- ❏ Important church certificates, ordinances

EDUCATION:
- ❏ Diplomas
- ❏ Class Schedule
- ❏ Map of school
- ❏ School Calendar
- ❏ Transcripts

EMPLOYMENT:
- ❏ Resume
- ❏ Employment info., contracts
- ❏ Retirement Pension, Profit Sharing
- ❏ Wage Statement/copy most recent paycheck stub
- ❏ Social Security Annual Statement

ESTATE PLANNING:
- ❏ Advanced Directive, Durable power of attorney for Health Care
- ❏ Financial Power of Attorney
- ❏ Revocable Living Trust & Will

- ❏ Final Instructions
- ❏ Documentation of Prepaid fees to cemetery/funeral home & contracts

FAMILY:
- ❏ Individual pictures of family members
- ❏ Child ID, DNA
- ❏ Adoption, Birth, Citizenship, Divorce, Marriage, Death Certificates
- ❏ Drivers License
- ❏ Military Records Service
- ❏ Passports
- ❏ Social Security # cards

FINANCIAL:
- ❏ Bank Name, Account # (deposit slips & business cards)
- ❏ Credit cards, credit card info. if lost phone #'s
- ❏ Investments – Annuities, Bonds, CD's, IRA'S, Stock certificates
- ❏ Mutual Funds, Money Markets
- ❏ Safe Deposit box #, location, list of contents
- ❏ Tax return

GENEALOGY:
- ❏ Backup/GEDCOM – on CD, floppy or flash drive
- ❏ Printed copy of index, pedigree chart & family group sheets

HOME:
- ❏ House & Car keys
- ❏ Food Storage Inventory
- ❏ Evacuation plan & escape routes
- ❏ Record of home repairs, maintenance etc.

HOUSING:
- ❏ Appraisal
- ❏ Mortgage statement
- ❏ Deeds
- ❏ Homeowners or Renters Insurance & coverage information
- ❏ Property taxes bill
- ❏ Land survey
- ❏ Title policy
- ❏ Home Inventory list, photos, video, & appraisals

INSURANCE:
- ❏ Disability Insurance
- ❏ Life Insurance Policy
- ❏ Long Term Care Insurance
- ❏ Medicare/Medicaid
- ❏ Travel Insurance

MEDICAL:
- ❏ Business cards Dr. Hospitals, Ortho, Veterinarian, etc.
- ❏ Dental Records (copies x-rays)
- ❏ Health, Dental & Vision Insurance Cards
- ❏ Copy of Health Insurance Policy
- ❏ Immunizations for each family member
- ❏ Medical History, list of Medications taken, copies of prescriptions for each family member
- ❏ Pet Records

PHOTOS:
- ❏ 3 hard copies of each person in family
- ❏ CD, Memory Stick or Negatives of important pictures & keepsakes
- ❏ Home and personal property photos for insurance purposes

Preparedness in Community
Read Hebrews 10:23-25

The values in this passage represent the way the Preparedness Peace course has been structured. We want to lean hard into Jesus, learn how to encourage and build up one another physically, spiritually, and emotionally, and do it all in the context of relationship.

1.) In verse 23, a key statement is made, "...hold unswervingly to the hope we profess, for He who promised is faithful." What promise does this verse speak of? Who is the author speaking to?

_____

_____

2.) Are there personal promises you feel that the Lord has given you and your family? A personal promise God has given me was clearly spoken to me in a prayer meeting one night. I felt this presence over my right shoulder, and from behind me, He said, "I am ***with*** you." It is amazing the power that the Word of God has in our lives. Sometimes he speaks things – implants them – into my heart and sometimes He highlights the Word and I know God is speaking that Scripture specifically to me. My most familiar way to hear from the Lord is in the wilderness... in the outdoors. Creation truly does reflect His glory (Psalm 19:1) and if we take the time to open our eyes and our ears, He will reveal Himself.

Write the promises the Lord has given you. If you don't feel you have a personal promise, ask the Lord for one – or more.

_____

_____

_____

3.) Why do you think the author says "...[to] not give up meeting together..." with people who spur you on in your walk with the Lord, who are like-minded, and who call out your destiny in Jesus? What is the value of gathering together? How has it helped you in your walk with the Lord?

_____

_____

_____

4.) He also says to "...spur one another on..." What does this mean and why do you think it is so essential to our walk with God?

_____

_____

Challenge: Ask the Lord for ways to encourage those around you this week. Cultivate life, encouragement, and boldness in your heart for the days to come.

The Lord Speaks About Things That Are to Come
Read Genesis 41:25-40

To refresh your memory, in chapters 39 and 40, Joseph has just spent several years in prison due to a false accusation by Potiphar's wife. While in prison, Joseph had great favor and was put in charge of all the men in prison, including Pharaoh's cupbearer and chief baker. One night, both men had dreams. Joseph told them that the Lord interprets dreams and correctly interpreted their dreams. Joseph asked that when they got out of prison that they would remember him and ask Pharaoh to release him. Both men were released from prison and their dreams came to pass, but both of them forgot about Joseph and two more years went by.

Then in one night, Pharaoh had two dreams that no one could interpret. Finally, the cupbearer remembers Joseph and tells Pharaoh he knows someone who might be able to interpret the dream. Joseph is summoned from prison, showers, shaves (probably the first time in over a year), and presents himself before Pharaoh. Pharaoh shares his dreams with him, and again, Joseph states, "I cannot do it, but God will give Pharaoh the answer he desires."

Regarding the crisis coming to Egypt, the Lord spoke in a dream to Pharaoh. Joseph, coming straight out of prison, accurately hears from the Lord and not only interprets Pharaoh's dream but gives **a plan of how to prepare a *nation* for seven years of famine.** Joseph was prepared to lead in the fire of prison, and all the while, maintained his heart before God.

1.) What three things stand out to you in this text?

_____

_____

2.) Does the Lord speak to you or anyone you know in dreams? Ask the Lord to speak to you and reveal Himself and His plans to you in your dreams.

_____

3.) In verse 25 it says, "God has revealed to Pharaoh what he is about to do." How do you feel about God bringing seven years of abundance and God bringing seven years of famine in Egypt? How does this fit into your image of God?

_____

_____

4.) God gave Joseph a seven year plan to prepare a nation. What was this plan? What is the Lord saying to you this week about how to prepare? Hear His voice. Trust Him and Obey.

_____

_____

_____

5.) In what ways does God reveal His goodness in this Scripture?

_____

_____

Joseph's Heart Before God
Read Genesis 41:25-40

And now let Pharaoh find a wise and discerning man, one in whom is the Spirit of God, and put him in charge. Let Pharaoh appoint commissioners over the land... they should collect food in the good years that will be used in the years of famine that will come upon Egypt. (Summary of Genesis 41:33-36)

It is important to note all of the *personal* preparation Joseph went through *before* he was ready to lead and have wisdom to lead a nation. Also consider that he came *straight* out of prison to interpret this dream. His heart must have been right before God. Good circumstances do not make you ready, but a right heart and knowledge of God make you ready to respond as the Lord leads you. Joseph was unjustly sentenced, abandoned, and forgotten by anyone who could release him, and having spent years of his life there, he emerges with a heart tender to the Lord, sensitive to His voice, and surrendered to His plans.

1.) Recount the seeming injustice of Joseph's life. What has happened to him to get him to this place?

_____

_____

How would you maintain your heart before the Lord if you were denied and sold by your family, left for dead, unjustly accused, forgotten about, and imprisoned for years?

_____

_____

2.) Can you look into your past and see a very hard, even unjust situation that you really suffered through? Has God used that specific situation in your life since then? How did that circumstance prepare you for something else in your life?

_____

_____

3.) Pharaoh knew exactly who he wanted to lead during these years of planning and famine. What does this speak to you about who will be needed to lead in the time of crisis?

_____

_____

_____

4.) Pharaoh, Joseph and all the people of the courts worked together to implement this plan. This was a sustained effort of planning, labor, trust, and follow through. Can you imagine seven years of planning and seven *years* of crisis? What will you and your team need to sustain relationship and effectiveness for both a short-term crisis and a longer-term crisis?

_____

_____

_____

Take Heed
Read Proverbs 27:12

1.) Do you see danger coming in the future? What type of danger? How does that affect your preparedness?

_____

_____

2.) List three consequences that you and your family could face if you are not prepared for a particular crisis.

_____

_____

_____

3.) Pray about these specific situations now. What did you find yourself praying about the most? What words came to mind? Do you think this is God leading you by His Holy Spirit?

_____

_____

_____

4.) 1 Thessalonians 5:14 says, "And we urge you, brothers, warn those who are idle, encourage the timid, help the weak, be patient with everyone." As you prepare and hear what the Lord is saying to you personally, will it shape the message you tell others about the times, seasons, and the need to prepare – physically, spiritually, emotionally?

_____

_____

_____

— Session Two —
Day Five Prayer Topic

Pray for _____

Spend this time praying for the situation your class has decided upon. Review your notes from last week. Ask God to continue to speak to you about specific people or details in this situation. What moves your heart as you pray? Maybe today it gets more specific. Stay with this focus and ask the Lord to reveal **more** *to you today.*

_____

_____

_____

_____

_____

WATER WISE & FOOD SENSE
SESSION THREE

NOTES

_____

_____

_____

_____

_____

_____

_____

_____

_____

_____

_____

_____

_____

_____

_____

_____

WATER WISE & FOOD SENSE

1.) Without air you can survive three _____, without water you can survive three _____, and without food you can survive three _____.

2.) It is recommended that you store a minimum of _____ gallon(s) of water per person per day.

3.) We take for granted how pure and plentiful water is to us now, it's hard to understand the importance of it when we are _____ it.

4.) 90 percent or more of the Earth's _____ water is impure.

5.) Water weighs _____ pounds per gallon.

6.) Remember, store what you _____, and eat what you store.

7.) In the Grab and Go Bag, it is good to have foods that are lightweight, _____ calorie, and _____ protein.

8.) Sustain a diet of _____ calories per day.

SESSION 3 SUMMARY

Clean, pure water is something that is very easy to take for granted. You turn on the faucet and poof – there it is. Take a shower, flush the toilet, wash your hands, water the plants, do the dishes and poof – there it is. You go outside to water the garden, wash the car, fill up the kiddy swimming pool. And what's even better, you can **drink** it!! And straight from the tap! It's clean, pure, slightly chlorinated, but immediately drinkable/potable.

What if that water source became contaminated? What if it was shut off completely? What if your primary water source was not available for days? Weeks? Or ever again? What would you do? Storage of water is one of the simplest but most neglected areas of emergency preparedness.

Water is **essential** for life. The human body contains anywhere from 55% to 78% water depending on body size. The brain is 70% water, lungs almost 90%, body fat is 10%, and bone has 22% water. And blood – essential for digestion, waste transport, and body temperature control – is about 83% water. Without water we will cease to exist. (Perlman)

WATER WISE

A person can only live three days without water. This is why it is essential that you have one gallon of water for consumption per person per day. The very minimum one should drink is 2.75 quarts per day, which equals 250 gallons per person per year for drinking water alone. This does not even begin to include hygiene, dishes, or laundry. You must store water now because not having enough water is a matter of life and death – children, pregnant women, and the elderly are especially at risk. When your body reaches the level of just 20% dehydrated, you can die. Reducing the amount of water in the body by this degree effects each of the bodily processes mentioned above and causes great stress on your body. Not to mention that dehydration can cause fatigue, headaches, dizziness, joint aches, mood swings, chapped skin, and can contribute to hypothermia and hyperthermia.

WE RECOMMEND:

WaterBrick
www.Bolands.ThriveLife.com

Storing water is very simple and inexpensive. With proper storage – clean containers, kept out of the heat and sunlight, and off of concrete floors (plastic containers stored on concrete causes the plastic to leach into the water) – water can have indefinite shelf life. Once you have water stored, it is advised that you empty it and refill it once per year. Daylight savings time is a good time to review and rotate all preparedness supplies.

Water Tips

- It is not necessary to treat water from a public water supply if it is already chlorinated.

- Storage places in crisis: bathtub, food grade 55 gallon barrel – if water is predicted to be unavailable or contaminated.

- Not enough water is a **good** reason to evacuate your home.

- Five gallon plastic water containers are available at army surplus, sporting goods, discount, and preparedness stores.

- Double bleach if water is cloudy. After adding proper dosage, stir and allow to stand about 30 minutes.

- We think that for storing water, the bleach route is easiest and cheapest. When outside of the home, and have a choice, a travel water filter is best. We recommend Sawyer or Katadyn.

- You can tie a piece of twine or rope around the neck of two liter containers, mount a 2×4 along storage walls and hook the liter bottles over nails on those boards. These can be run high next to the ceiling to use otherwise wasted space in storage areas.

- Cardboard is a great barrier between concrete and bottles.

Step 5
Fill, date, and store

Possible storage locations: Bathroom cupboards, backs of closets, corners of shelves, bookshelves, behind or under beds, corners of kitchen cabinets, food storage room.

Step 4
Treat water if necessary

Use unscented bleach

WATER		BLEACH
1	Quart	2 drops
½	Gallon	4 drops
1	Gallon	8 drops
5	Gallons	0.5 teaspoon
55	Gallons	5.5 teaspoons

Step 3
Clean containers

Clean them with dishwashing soap and water, including the original caps. Rinse thoroughly. Soda bottles only: Combine 1 tsp bleach with 1 quart of water and swish it around the entire container. Rinse thoroughly.

Step 2
Collect or purchase containers

Good Storage Containers: Gallons of filtered water, one or two liter soda bottles, juice bottles, mouthwash bottles, Gatorade bottles, Pedialyte bottles, barrels (food or water grade). DO NOT USE milk containers, or anything metal.

Step 1
Calculate how much water you should store

1 gallon/person/day
For drinking water only
3 gallons/person/day includes hygiene, dishes
Dogs: 1 gallon/day
Cats: 1 pint/day

Gray Water is any water source that is not pure. Gray water – from the rain barrel or from a stream – must be purified or filtered for drinking. Three methods to purify gray water include boiling water for two minutes, using iodine tablets dissolved in the water, or using a water filter to clean the water for drinking. You should have gray water sources identified before a disaster strikes. Get a local topographic map and seek out water sources in your area. Ponds, lakes, creeks, and rivers offer urban solutions for accessing more water. Rain barrels are an excellent gray water source that may be used directly to water gardens, trees, or yard, and to flush toilets. Remember all gray water must be treated before it is used to drink, cook, brush teeth, wash hands, face, or dishes; these activities require pure water to avoid waterborne illness.

Whatever route you choose to take with treating and storing water, the most important thing is to ***get to it today***!

Cool Water Facts!

* Use dishwashing soap bottles, liquid laundry soap bottles, and liquid soap bottles too. After you use it all up, don't rinse it out. Fill with water and label bottle "soapy water." That way you will have it to use for sanitation and not have to use precious drinking water for washing dishes, cleaning, personal hygiene, etc.

Cool Fact:
* You can improve the taste of stored water by pouring it back and forth between two containers. This will add oxygen to the water and improve its taste.

Things you'll need:
* Containers
* Dishwashing soap
* Non-scented household bleach
* Permanent marker

FOOD SENSE

Food is important, but not as important as water. You could live for three weeks without any food. We do not encourage this, but we pray you take comfort in knowing this.

The Prep Steps diagram helps us visualize the importance and the process and progression of food storage. This course is about establishing a *basic* foundation, but as you can see in the Prep Steps diagram, there is reason to be prepared further. This chart helps you determine the types of foods you should purchase based on your preparedness goal at this time. Our hope is that you will move up the prep steps in the weeks and years to come.

As you establish or build on your foundation of preparedness, you will see that building food storage for your family can be rather simple. There are so many different ways to prepare as it relates to food. Personal preferences and dietary needs should be considered as you make these important plans for your family. Make sure you store enough food for every member of your family (including pets)! Specifically, you need to be able to maintain a diet of 2,000-3,000 calories per day. Do the math now – consider portions X meals X number of people in your family – and *buy* accordingly. Don't forget you need to do this for your Home Emergency Supplies, Grab and Go Bags, and Car Kit. A good way to do this is to start buying a little extra of the foods you eat every trip to the store. **This helps you to store what you eat and eat what you store.** Again, this food needs to be labeled with the storage date and rotated in a way that older items are used first and newer items placed in the back. Oh, and did I mention that you should also include *comfort* foods in your emergency supplies? Having foods, gum, or candies that bring comfort are very nice to have in difficult times.

GRAB AND GO BAG	CAR KIT	HOME KIT
- Clif Bars	- 3600 calorie bars	- Canned food
- 3600 calorie bars	- Granola bars	- Freeze dried food
- Granola bars	- MREs	- Dehydrated food
- Ready-to-Eat Meals (MREs)	- GORP	- Bulk food
- Good Old Raisins and Peanuts (GORP)	- Jerky	
- Jerky		
- Tuna packs with crackers (aseptic pkg)		

THE PREP STEPS

SUSTAINED
(PERPETUAL SURVIVAL)
SEEDS, GARDENING, ALT ENERGY, NATURAL WATER SOURCE...
TOTAL GOV. COLLAPSE, LIVING OFF GRID

3 MONTH
BULK STAPLE FOODS, LARGE FUEL SUPPLY, WATER COLLECTION/FILTRATION, HUNTING...
HURRICANE, EARTHQUAKE, FOOD SHORTAGES

3 WEEK
BULK FOODS, BULK COOKING FUEL, COOKING SUPPLIES, WATER BARRELS...
TORNADO, CIVIL UNREST, LONG POWER OUTAGES

3 DAY
REGULAR KITCHEN SUPPLIES OF FOOD, GALLONS OF WATER, POSSIBLE HEAT SOURCE...
POWER OUTAGE, WINTER STORM

GRAB AND GO BAG FOODS

The foods you purchase for your home will be very different than the foods you purchase for your grab and go bags. Weight is important to consider when packing bags that you will carry. The varied methods of food packaging makes packing for mobility easy. Here are some examples: aseptic packaging for tuna, salmon, and chicken in Tetra Paks, others include Clif Bars (my personal favorite), granola bars, dried fruit and nuts, beef jerky, and high calorie and protein emergency food bars. These take up very little space, produce very little waste, and have a substantial shelf life. Freeze-Dried foods work well and are very shelf stable. MREs are not found at the grocery store but are another great source of nutrient rich ready-to-eat foods. We do not recommend carrying canned goods or dehydrated foods. Canned foods are heavy and require a can opener. Dehydrated foods require preparation in order to eat them. Please note: all of these items need to be consumed with ample amounts of water.

WE RECOMMEND:

Meals Ready to Eat (MRE)
Bolands.ThriveLife.com

Your car kit will probably have similar types of food as your grab and go bag but in this case weight is of slightly less importance. Do be mindful of the effect that time and temperature play on the shelf life of foods – even MREs.

High temperatures erode shelf life more quickly than one would think. Keep this in mind with foods kept in a car. The other side to the same coin is when foods are stored well in cool temperatures and kept in dry, airtight containers, most foods will last longer than many people think. Rotation is the key. Take preventative measures to keep insects under control. Store items well and keep storage areas clean.

The types of foods you eat and the amount of foods you eat are very important in disaster. Long shelf life and nutritional value are equally important. Just because Twinkies last ten years, does not mean they make a good staple disaster plan food. Remember the importance of fiber, protein, carbohydrates, and healthy fats. Vitamins are a great way to supplement produce – which might not be so readily available – unless it's growing in your garden. It is important that, even in crisis, your diet contain all food groups!

STORING HARD CHEESE

1.) *Take cheese out of wrapper.*

2.) *Dip in hot paraffin, let cool and dry, then dip again.*

3.) *Do this at least four times. Five times is better.*

4.) *If the wax should become chipped at any time, just redip.*

5.) *Store on shelf in cool dark place, a basement shelf works well.*

6.) *Turn every once in a while and it will keep almost forever.*

Remember, storing up Scripture is as important as storing up water and food.

WE RECOMMEND:

Sawyer Complete Water Purifier System at .02 Microns
1 Million Gallons Guaranteed
Sawyer Point Zero Two Purifier
www.Bolands.ThriveLife.com

Choose three or more of the questions below and share the answers in your group now.
*Recomended discussion questions

1.) How much food and water do you have stored currently?
Days of food _____   Gallons of water _____

2.) Do you feel like you are truly aware of how much water you use and how dependent you are upon it coming from the tap?

❏ Yes   ❏ No

3.)* Consider how much water you use **now** (and all the reasons), then calculate how many gallons of water your family needs **per day** to survive and write it here:
_____ gallons

Share with the group ideas you have for water storage including types of bottles and locations for storage.
_____
_____

4.) Do you currently have a water filtration/purification system or strategy? What is it?
❏ Yes   ❏ No
My water filter/purification strategy: _____
_____

5.) What is your goal for food storage?
❏ 3 Days   ❏ 3 Weeks   ❏ 3 Months

6.)* Discuss why different types of foods with different types of packaging are necessary as we move up the Prep Steps. (See Prep Step graphic in this session)
_____
_____

7.)* Considering your families' preferences, what are the top priority food items you will store?
_____
_____
_____

Biblical Focus and Discussion

Preview and discuss the verses to be studied during the week. Read each scripture aloud as a group and discuss first impressions, any current or past revelation on that verse, and pray together that God would speak to you as you study His Scripture this week.

SESSION THREE | DAY ONE

Mattew 14:15-20 "...*This is a remote place, and it is already getting late. Send the crowds away so they can go to the villages and buy themselves some food.' Jesus replied, 'They do not need to go away, **you give them something to eat**.' 'We have here only five loaves of bread and two fish,' they answered. 'Bring them here to me' he said... Taking the five loaves and the two fish and looking up to heaven, he **gave thanks** and broke the loaves. Then He gave them to the disciples... [and] the people... and all ate and were satisfied.*" [Emphasis added]

SESSION THREE | DAY TWO

Mark 8:4 "*His disciples answered, 'But where in this remote place can anyone get enough bread to feed them?'*"

SESSION THREE | DAY THREE

Mark 8:17-21 "*Why are you talking about having no bread? Do you still not see or understand? Are your hearts hardened? Do you have eyes but fail to see, and ears but fail to hear? And don't you remember?*"... "*Do you still not understand?*"

SESSION THREE | DAY FOUR

Isaiah 55:2b "*Listen, listen to me, and eat what is good, and your soul will delight in the richest of fare.*"

Psalms 33:18-19 "*But the eyes of the Lord are on those who fear Him, on those whose hope is in His unfailing love, to deliver them from death and keep them alive in famine.*"

SESSION THREE | DAY FIVE

Prayer Focus: _____

Share with your group what God is highlighting to you about this topic in your prayer time.

YouTube:	History Channel, After Armageddon, Sessions 5-6
Resource:	http://www.hgtv.com/gardening/conserve-water-with-a-rain-barrel/index.html
Website:	users.htcomp.net/prep/
Book:	*Prayers To Strengthen Your Inner Man: Personal Prayer Lists* by Mike Bickle
Scripture:	Exodus 16

1.) How many total gallons does your family need? _____
How many days/week will it last? _____
At eight pounds per gallon, how much does all that water weigh? _____

2.) Water is necessary for survival. Store enough water for your family for at least three days. (If you have already stored three days worth, *increase* the amount that you have.)

❏ I have made an effort to increase the total amount of water I store.

For the benefit of other team members, bring to class a brief, personal report on the storage bottle types you used and the location(s) where you stored your water.

_____

_____

_____

3.) Using the Prep Step Inventory in the Lists section, designate at least three days of food prepared for your home emergency supplies, grab and go bag, and car kit. Purchase or designate food in your pantry to be used for these kits. (If you have already achieved this, build on what you have *this* week.)

❏ I met my food preparation goal
❏ This one is still in process

Family Plans and Documents:
4.) You should spend a majority of your time this week preparing the documents. This week, **finish** gathering all documents to be copied (refer to list in Session 2). Identify to whom you will give each document and how many copies you will need of each document. Don't forget, you will need one copy of **all** documents for the family safe or firebox.

❏ I finished gathering all my docs
❏ I know how many copies I need of each document
❏ I'm still waiting on my son, daughter, wife, husband, grandmother, veterinarian, bank, insurance agent, or out of town contact to get me what I need.

5.) Complete ZebGear's Serious Preparedness Challenge: Choosing the Right Foods on the next page.

6.) Read and respond to this session's daily devotionals beginning on the following pages.

ZEB GEAR SERIOUS PREPAREDNESS CHALLENGE
CHALLENGE: CHOOSING THE RIGHT FOODS

Here's your challenge:

1. Make a list of special dietary needs for yourself and your family.
2. Make a list of foods you and your family enjoys eating or are a part of your regular diet. This can include items like milk, cheese, and eggs for example.
3. What's your food storage goal...enough food for 1 week, 1 month, or 1 year? (We recommend 30 days to 1 year)
4. What are some foods you or your family would consider comfort foods. For example, Jell-O, brownies, cookies, etc. A disaster can cause radical change; foods that you are familiar with can help to normalize the situation.
5. Determine the shortest shelf-life you want in your food storage. Is it 1 month, 1 year, 5 years, etc.? If you selected one year for example, your food selections will have an expiration date at least one year from the day you purchase them.
6. Do you want to package your own bulk foods or purchase them packaged for you?
7. Determine what freeze-dried meals your whole family would enjoy.

Serious Preparedness Challenge Scoring	YES 1 Point	NO 0 Points
Did you make a list of special dietary needs?		
Did you make a list of foods you enjoy eating?		
Did you write down your food storage goal? (1 week – 1 year)		
Did you make a list of some comfort foods?		
Did you determine the shortest shelf-life you will use in your food storage plan?		
Did you determine if you want to package your own bulk foods or purchase them packaged for you?		
Did you investigate freeze-dried meals your whole family would enjoy?		
Column Totals		

Scoring:
0 – 1: It will be important for you to repeat and complete this challenge.
2 – 3: It will be important for you to repeat and complete this challenge.
4 – 5: If you received a zero in an area that is not important to your food storage plan, you are ready to begin building your food storage.
6 – 7: You have an excellent plan to begin building your food storage.

This challenge will have helped you start a list of food items to purchase and how to purchase food that will fit your requirements for specific dietary needs and a minimum shelf-life. You're off to a great start! Now you can begin to build your extended food storage.

May Faith Rise Up
Read Matthew 14:13-21

I love this passage because it represents so much of the physical, emotional, and spiritual dynamics that we will experience when faced with great need in the context of disaster. The need in this story is overwhelming. The disciples recognize their inability to ever provide for all these people.

No matter how much food and water you store, there will not be enough food to feed **all** who have need. But just like in the story with the disciples, Jesus hears your petition, and says "**You** feed them." In the authority given to you by Jesus – "you feed them." I believe a major key to seeing food multiplied is to do what Jesus did. He took the bread and the fish that were brought to Him, he looked to heaven, **gave thanks**, and then broke the bread and gave it away. In each of these stories, "all ate and were satisfied" with leftovers! As we offer what we have to the Lord, give thanks and give it away... the Lord will continue to provide what is needed. Place what you have before the Lord, believing that He still multiplies what we give Him, and watch with great expectation all that He will do.

1.) Have you ever been in a situation where the need was overwhelming and you wanted to do more but you just couldn't? How did that make you feel?

_____

_____

_____

2.) Just like in the story with the disciples, Jesus hears your petition, and says "**You** feed them." Really? How many times have you heard the Lord ask you to do something but doubted that you could? How do you get to that place where you believe God to do what He does through you?

_____

_____

_____

3.) What if, with simple and huge faith, we offered what we have to the Lord, looked to heaven, gave thanks for every bit, and then gave it away? Oh to see with my eyes and my hands the multiplication of food! What do you long to see God do in you and through you?

_____

_____

_____

4.) Pray today for faith to rise up in your heart. Ask God to prepare you now for the mighty things He will do as you **lean** on Him in the places of need that will arise.

_____

_____

_____

He Reminds Us
Read Mark 8:1-8

Shortly after feeding the 5,000 the disciples find themselves in a similar situation needing to feed 4,000. Again, in Mark 8:4 they ask Jesus, "...where in this remote place can anyone get enough bread to feed them?" And again, He takes what they have, gives thanks, breaks the bread and gives it away. We are much like the disciples, forgetting the ways God has moved in our own lives, forgetting his faithfulness and the way He has provided for us and others.

1.) Have you ever seen the Lord provide in a specific way in your life, but when the *same* situation came up again struggled with doubt and fear that He would provide? Explain that situation here.

_____

_____

_____

2.) In Exodus 34:6, The Lord describes Himself to Moses, "The Lord, the Lord, the compassionate and gracious God, slow to anger, abounding in love and faithfulness..." How have you experienced God in this way in your life, especially as it relates to forgetting the things He has done or doubting what He will do in the future?

_____

_____

_____

3.) Are there any areas of preparedness or crisis that you fear the Lord will not provide for you and your family? Write them here and take them to the Lord in prayer now. Listen for His response – promises or comfort that you will be able to carry with you every day.

_____

_____

_____

── Session Three ──
Day Three Devotional

The Compassionate and Gracious God
Read Mark 8:14-21

The disciples and Jesus set out on another trip and then realize they only have one loaf of bread. Anticipating their weak, human response, Jesus says in verse 15, "Watch out for the yeast of the Pharisees and that of Herod." Yet they still worry because they only have one loaf of bread and finally Jesus says, "Why are you talking about having no bread? Do you still not see or understand? Are your hearts hardened? Do you have eyes but fail to see, and ears but fail to hear? And don't you remember? ...Do you still not understand?"

1.) Here is a paraphrased conversation between Jesus and the disciples: Jesus: "Watch out for the yeast (doubt and unbelief) of the Pharisees!" The disciples talk together about what He just told them, misinterpret his comment, and conclude "it is because we have no bread."

In this journey of learning to hear and understand the voice of the Lord there is *no* pressure to always get it right. Cultivate the ability to hear and understand what the Lord is speaking to you.

Ask the Lord to speak to you tonight and record what you hear Him say.

_____

_____

_____

2.) A really fun and encouraging activity is to ask the Lord what He thinks about someone else. Not only will He share the amazing things He sees in this person, but you get to be His voice and speak that encouragement into their life. Try it now. Ask the Lord what He thinks about your spouse or your child or your boss or your best friend. Write what He says here:

_____

_____

_____

3.) Back to the misinterpreted conversation in question #1, Jesus knows they don't understand and continues to speak to them, continues to explain it to them. God *loves* to reveal Himself and loves for us to seek Him out as well. Do you think that God gets frustrated with you? Do you feel like He never gives you a straight answer? Reread verses 20-21 and write your response to Jesus explaining Himself to the disciples yet not spelling it out word for word. Why do you think He does this?

_____

_____

_____

4.) The Lord loves to speak to His people. In John 16:14, Jesus is speaking about the Spirit of Truth and says "He [Holy Spirit] will bring glory to me by taking from what is mine and making it known to you." The Lord receives *glory* when you hear from the Holy Spirit! Do you *know* how much the Lord loves to speak to *you*? Write your thoughts about this here: (and if the answer is no, ask the Lord to show you!)

_____

_____

_____

5.) The bottom line of all this is that Jesus *can* do the impossible! Three times the disciples were faced with not having enough and three times the Lord provided for them miraculously. Jesus is alive and He is the same yesterday, today, and tomorrow, and we must *know* Him in this way. Do you want to believe God for miracles to happen in your life? Is there anything that holds you back from believing that it is still possible today? Write your answer and your prayer about it here:

_____

_____

_____

The Great Invitation

Read and meditate on the following verses: Isaiah 55:1-3, Psalm 33:18-19, and Psalm 111:5

1.) What is the common theme in these three verses?

_____

_____

_____

2.) Reread Isaiah 55:1-3. This passage addresses those people with nothing, the ones with great need, and those that have everything, feasting on things that will never truly satisfy. His instructions and His promise are the same to both parties. What **are** His instructions? What **is** His promise?

_____

_____

_____

3.) In Psalm 33:18 it says, "...the eyes of the Lord are on those who fear Him, on those whose hope is in His **unfailing love**" [emphasis added]. I find it so interesting that the author does not say: Hope in God's faithfulness, goodness, or strength. He says "...**hope** in His **unfailing love**." Let this resound in your heart. What does this mean? What does this look like in your life?

_____

_____

_____

Pray for _____

Spend this time praying for the situation your class has decided upon. Ask God to continue to speak to you about this situation. What moves your heart as you pray today? Even if you feel like He says something unusual, jot it down, pray through it and share with your team next session.

_____

_____

_____

_____

_____

POWER ALLEY

SESSION FOUR

NOTES

_____

_____

_____

_____

_____

_____

_____

_____

_____

_____

_____

_____

_____

_____

_____

_____

POWER ALLEY
EMERGENCY POWER AND LIGHTING

1.) Lighting in a power outage is not that difficult, it just takes a little _____.

2.) Flashlights with fresh batteries should be in an easy to find _____ that everyone in the home knows about.

3.) Train your _____ to learn to safely handle flashlights and other resources you plan to use in the event of no electricity.

4.) Careful use of all heat and fire sources is a must in a disaster situation because _____.
Do you have a fire extinguisher?

5.) The best way to prolong the life of the food in the refrigerator and freezer is to keep the _____ closed.

6.) BONUS QUESTION (not included in video)
Regarding concern for the life of the food in fridge, a golden rule is "If in doubt, _____ it out!"

SESSION 4 SUMMARY

*W**ant to know if you are ready for a power outage? Turn off the power and find out. Electricity – or the lack thereof – is not a hard thing to plan for if you understand how much you rely on it.***

There are many things to consider and plan for in the event of no power: alternative light, heat, cooking, food in refrigerator and freezer, communication, and entertainment.

ALTERNATIVE LIGHT SOURCES

There are a number of light sources including flashlights, Maglites (also a good weapon), headlamps (really great for hands free), oil lanterns, 100 hour candles, and glow sticks. You will find that different types of light are best for different purposes, for example, grab and go bags need lightweight, hands free, type of lights.

**Solar Link Scorpion
Weather Radio/Light**
www.Bolands.ThriveLife.com

In your home, you can use a variety of lighting solutions. **Make sure that you strategically place flashlights in all necessary locations.** The MacTiernan's hang flashlights on the back of every door. The Boland's have a combination of flashlights, candles with lighters, and headlamps placed in strategic places around their home. **Regardless of the lighting plan you make, be sure that everyone – including children – in your home knows where the lights are stored and how to use them safely.** Light solutions are easy to put in place, it just requires a little planning.

BATTERIES

Most types of flashlights require batteries. Plan ahead! Rechargeable batteries are best. You will need a hand crank or solar charger – many weather radios operate with a hand crank and will charge other devices too. Always have backup batteries available as well.

CHARGING THINGS

The ability to charge things – cell phones, computers, HAM radios, batteries – is very important. There are different options depending upon how much you want to spend. Hand crank chargers are of minimum cost and then there are solar chargers at the other end of the cost spectrum. Both are very effective but very different in operation and output. Auto inverters work well for short-term disasters while you have battery power and fuel in your vehicle. The ability to charge necessary items when you need them is of great value. Be sure to familiarize yourself with the output of each type of charger and make your charger decision based on your output needs.

HEATING AND COOLING YOUR HOME

Depending upon where you live, considerations for heating and cooling your home are also important. Cooling your home is rather difficult without electricity though they do make battery-powered fans and screens for windows and doors. In areas of the country that are colder, a lack of heat can be life-threatening. Heating the entire house may be a difficult task, but it is very possible to section off a room in your home using blankets, tarps, rope, tape, and clothespins to heat a smaller area. Extra sleeping bags and blankets will be a nice addition to these supplies. If you have a fireplace or wood stove, it would be smart to build your warming room around it. Both the fireplace and wood stove need to be maintained properly, clean, and safe to use. Don't forget to store firewood and kindling (some people are keeping their junk mail for just this purpose). If you do not have a fireplace or stove, another good source of heat is the freestanding kerosene heater.

COOKING

A nice, warm meal is no small thing in the context of crisis. The types of foods you have stored and the type of preparations you have made regarding preparing meals will determine the amount of cooking you are able to do. If you have a gas stove, you may need to light it manually, but other than that it will not be affected when there is no electricity. For those of you who do not have gas stoves, you could cook over the fire in your fireplace or in an open air fire outdoors. There are wood stoves, camp stoves, and dutch ovens that can be used outdoors. It is really encouraging to see all of the cooking solutions available online. One of our favorite stoves is the Volcano Collapsible Propane grill. It can be fueled with propane, charcoal, or wood. Be sure to choose a cooking solution that you are comfortable with and can use on a regular basis rather than just in crisis. It is so fun to learn that you can cook – and even bake amazing foods like pizza – on an outdoor fire.

Sun Oven
Bolands.ThriveLife.com

Alternative cooking methods also require proper utensils. You can't use the same utensils and pots on a live fire that you would use on your stove in the kitchen. Cast iron is a great thing to invest in (or find at a garage sale) now. If using a camp stove of some sort, you will want to use pots and utensils that are compatible with the size and weight limits of your camp stove. The point is, you can't wait until disaster strikes to figure it out. Go camping, borrow friends' stoves, and figure out what you like and then *use* it often.

FIRE SAFETY

Fire seems to be a hot topic as we talk about cooking, heating, and lighting. You need ways to start fires – matches, lighters, flint – and put out fires, a *fire extinguisher* is a must! **Safety is of utmost importance in a crisis situation because there is a good chance that YOYO! YOU'RE ON YOUR OWN!** It could be due to weather and downed trees that emergency services are unable to reach you or maybe communications are down and you cannot reach them. Oftentimes in crisis, the emergency services are overwhelmed and response times are slow at best. For this reason, you must be on high alert while using fire to cook, heat, or light your home. Lighting is an ongoing need while the power is out. If you do choose to use candles, you need to take precautions to keep them from burning too hot or too close to other objects. You must remember to blow them out. Many people suggest not using candles at all, but the bottom line is that you will use what you have. Know how to use it safely and have a fire extinguisher in place to deal with emergencies. Practice using your

fire extinguisher before an event occurs and teach anyone else in the house who might have to use it as well.

Fire Extinguisher
Bolands.ThriveLife.com

ENTERTAINMENT

During a power outage – whether short-term or long-term – those members of your family who typically rely on TV, the Internet, or electronic games (even on the iPhone) for entertainment will find themselves bored and anxious in a very short time. It is a good idea to have choice family games or activities in place for each member of your family to keep everyone entertained. Don't forget to put activities for children in the safe room.

REFRIGERATOR/FREEZER/FOOD

The food in your refrigerator and freezer is of significant value whether it is packed full of food or simply holds things that are important to your health – like medications. You want to be able to maintain a cold temperature inside the unit as long as possible. Common sense goes a long way but is harder to enforce when there are children around who are used to getting in the fridge when they feel like it. **A couple of tips to help keep doors closed and cool air in are: tape the doors shut, tie a ribbon around the handles, or put a big sign that says Do Not Open on the door.** These tools will help everyone remember to think twice before opening the doors and letting more cold air out.

If it is a local disaster and you can get out of your area, go buy ice! Using an ice chest to store food has the potential to extend food by approximately one week. It is helpful to know in advance where you would buy ice. Keep in mind, prices can skyrocket after a crisis hits so plan funds accordingly.

To ensure the safety of your food, it is good to have a refrigerator/freezer thermometer. This will allow you to monitor the temperature inside the unit and make an informed decision about what to do with your food. If you are concerned about the food spoiling, you need to cook it or eat it right away. **The golden rule when dealing with food is "If in doubt, *Throw it out!*"** Especially in the context of crisis, an ILLNESS is worse than having to toss out some food because it is in a questionable state. Pay attention to the odors and colors of food and if concerned, then ***toss it***.

GENERATOR

A generator is not necessary for basic preparedness, but of course is great to have for more long-term situations. It is still important to note that you currently rely on a lot more energy than an average generator can give you.

Let's talk sizes of generators. These are generalized numbers regarding watts and what you can charge, but will give a helpful estimation. A heavy extension cord run outside to a 2,500 watt or larger generator will keep a few lights on, batteries recharged, and the refrigerator on. 5,000 watts will keep the whole house in power but with no air conditioning. 8,500 watts should supply the entire house with all you need and run the air conditioner.

Even with a generator, you do not know how long the crisis could last and therefore need to take into consideration the amount of fuel you have stored, how much fuel the generator uses, and what is truly necessary to maintain important items in your home. If you are only concerned with charging essential items, one or two hours of generator use each evening about the time you need the lights should be sufficient. If you wish to keep the food in the refrigerator cool, then you may have to run the generator twice a day. Monitor your thermometers to determine usage. Even if you have the watts and the fuel and feel like you can run 24/7, we would strongly encourage you to ration usage until you know the scope and severity of the situation.

Lithium Ion Silent Power Station 1000
Bolands.ThriveLife.com

Regarding fuel storage, gas is good for about a year with fuel additive, but be careful it could be against local codes to store fuel. Be sure to research and follow all safety regulations for fuel storage according to your Homeowner Variance and ***never, never, never*** run your generator indoors!

PREPARING CHILDREN

Power Alley brings up some exciting topics. The skills necessary to thrive without electricity are engaging and require practice. Especially where children are involved, it is very important to engage children with each one of the resources needed during these times. Everything from lights to fire to cooking and food. You need to create opportunities for them to learn how to safely operate and interact with these resources so that in the event of a disaster, they have the understanding that this is ***not*** play and are able to respect and even participate in serving the family in these ways.

BASIC PREPAREDNESS

We, the authors of Preparedness Peace, understand that the principles discussed in this section are basic in nature. We intentionally want to focus on the basics as they are often overlooked. Some of the more simple strategies to prepare your home are still necessary even though massive generators or solar panels are now available. We unabashedly have the objective to get all people to achieve a ***basic*** level of preparedness that they can build on for many years to come.

Choose three or more of the questions below and share the answers in your group now.
*Recommended discussion questions

1.) Describe your experience during a recent power outage.

_____

_____

_____

2.) Share your favorite alternative light source and why. (Get excited about gear!)

_____

_____

3.)* Brainstorm together ways that you can train your children/team to use preparedness resources properly: maybe through a game, a family adventure in the dark, camping, etc.

_____

_____

4.)* What does YOYO mean to you? You're On Your Own, in terms of no police, medical, or fire protection. Discuss the possible ramifications for your family in a crisis situation.

_____

_____

_____

5.) How dependent are you on outside information sources – phone, Internet, email, TV, or newspaper? All of these sources could be unavailable during a power outage. How will this lack of information and communication affect you?

_____

_____

6.) Approximately what is the dollar value of the food in your refrigerator and freezer? What might be your strategy to preserve/use this food before it goes bad?

_____

_____

7.) Considering extreme temperatures, share your strategies regarding heating/cooling your home and the possibility of owning and operating a generator.

_____

_____

(PEACE) Biblical Focus and Discussion

Preview and discuss the verses to be studied during the week. Read each scripture aloud as a group and discuss first impressions, any current or past revelation on that verse, and pray together that God would speak to you as you study His Scripture this week.

SESSION FOUR | DAY ONE

Revelation 1:12-13 *"I turned around to see the voice that was speaking to me. And when I turned I saw seven golden lampstands, and among the lampstands was someone 'like a son of man...'"*

SESSION FOUR | DAY TWO

Revelation 1:17-18 *"When I saw him, I fell at his feet as though dead. Then he placed his right hand on me and said: 'Do not be afraid. I am the First and the Last. I am the Living One; I was dead, and behold I am alive for ever and ever! And I hold the keys of death and Hades.'"*

SESSION FOUR | DAY THREE

Psalm 54:4 *"Surely God is my help; the Lord is the one who sustains me."*

Psalm 3:4-6 *"I call out to the LORD, and he answers me from his holy mountain. I lie down and sleep; I wake again, because the LORD sustains me. I will not fear though tens of thousands assail me on every side."*

SESSION FOUR | DAY FOUR

Mark 6:30-31 *"The apostles gathered around Jesus and reported to him all they had done and taught. Then, because so many people were coming and going that they did not even have a chance to eat, he said to them, 'Come with me by yourselves to a quiet place and get some rest.'"*

SESSION FOUR | DAY FIVE

Prayer Focus: _____

Share with your group what God is highlighting to you about this topic in your prayer time.

YouTube: History Channel, After Armageddon, Sessions 7-8

Websites: www.Bolands.ThriveLife.com

Challenge: Go without electricity for one evening

Scripture: Study Isaiah 11:1-3

Book: *How to Survive the End of the World as We Know It: Tactics, Techniques, and Technologies for Uncertain Times* by James Wesley Rawles

1.) For times of extended power outage, customize a food plan that is unique to your family for the items in your freezer and fridge. Be sure to consider special dietary requirements, medications, etc.

_____

_____

2.) Create and implement your lighting plan. Strategically place light sources of your choosing – flashlights, lanterns, headlamps, batteries, candles, matches, lighters, and fire extinguishers – throughout your home. Be sure everyone in your family knows the location and proper handling of each resource.

❏ I have competed my lighting plan.

3.) Devise a strategy of how you will heat and cool your home without electricity. If it's within your budget, execute that strategy.

_____

_____

4.) **Family Plans and Documents**: *Copy* all necessary documents (refer to the checklist in Session 2 for documents you chose to copy), package them in waterproof bags, and place all documents where you want them to be – a firebox, your grab and go bags, etc.

❏ I have copied all necessary documents.

5.) Plan a date this week (or in the *near* future) to go without electricity in your home for one evening.

Write the date of execution here : _____

6.) Identify and list below all the things you rely on electricity for in your daily life. Bring this list to the next session.

_____   _____   _____
_____   _____   _____
_____   _____   _____
_____   _____   _____

7.) Assemble your Home Emergency Supplies and your Car Kit using the Lists provided in the Lists section of this workbook.

8.) Read and respond to this session's daily devotionals on the following pages. Seek the Lord as you read through the devotionals.

One like a Son of Man
Revelation 1:11-18

Today and tomorrow's devotionals are a little different than the other devotionals in this workbook. This will be great for you creative, outside of the box people. Engage with the text, know there are no wrong answers, and expect to see something you have never seen about the person of Jesus Christ.

1.) One should not overlook the opportunity to behold the person of Jesus as described in chapter one. Reread John's description of this One "like the Son of Man" in verses 12-16 of chapter one. What stands out to you in this description? Why? _____

_____

_____

2.) I want you to take these specific descriptions – His eyes were like blazing fire, His feet were like bronze glowing in a furnace, and his voice was like the sound of rushing waters – and write what that means to you. For example, "His voice was like the sound of rushing water." This says to me that God's voice is powerful, it draws your attention and even when you are distant from it, you can still hear it, faint as it may be. Once you get too far away, you cannot hear it anymore. I see this come into play with my relationship with Jesus. When I can hear him and see Him, I want more and want to be closer. When I get too far from Him, I can't hear Him.

Choose one of the things that stood out to you above. Dig into it. What is it saying about Jesus? What does that attribute represent to you? _____

_____

_____

_____

3.) Choose one additional attribute from this description and do the same thing you did above. Explore the meaning of the description, make it personal. How do you relate to and understand personally this characteristic of Jesus?

_____

_____

_____

4.) This description of Jesus is amazing and powerful. John specifies that among the lampstands was someone like the son of man. This man, Jesus, is in the midst of His lampstands – The Churches. He is the one that gives all light, life, power, and love. This verse reveals His presence ***with*** us, amidst us, empowering the Church. How would your life change if you could ***see*** this "One like the Son of Man" standing next to you at all times?

_____

_____

_____

One like a Son of Man
Read Revelation 1:12-18

1.) In verse 12, John says he "...turned around to see the voice that was speaking to me. And when I turned I saw seven golden lampstands, and among the lampstands was someone 'like a son of man...'" Jesus is the light of the world. We receive all the light, love, and power that we carry from Jesus. We do not have light on our own, but must get it from the source. Given this truth, doesn't it make sense that we find out how to sustain power to this lamp? And why is it important that He stands among them? Write all your thoughts about this here. Remember, there are no wrong answers.

_____
_____
_____
_____

2.) This makes our role on the Earth very significant. If Jesus is the only source of light, love, and power, and He has chosen you to be His lampstand, you must continue to get or receive this light, love, and power but also continue to *be* the light, love, and power to those around you. What does this look like in your life? What is the key to a being a brighter light? And how does increasing your light affect the lives of others?

_____
_____
_____
_____

3.) Read Revelation 1:17-18 again. Stop right now and imagine Jesus doing this to you. Here is an enactment of what He would do if you were standing in front of Him now. He puts His hand on your shoulder, looks you in the eyes, and says "Do not be afraid, child. I am the First and the Last. I was the counselor at God's side when He created the Earth, I have overcome death, and hold *life* in the palm of my hand. My child, you have nothing to fear." Receive these words into your heart and your spirit now.

This is Truth and this is *power*. Plug into this source.

May we never lose sight of who Jesus is. What did you experience as you read these words, imagined Jesus speaking them to you, and then received them?

_____
_____
_____
_____

The One Who Sustains Us
Read Psalm 54:4; Psalm 3:4-6

I don't believe that David – the author of both of these psalms – always knew the Lord as His help and the One who sustained him. I believe that David's journey through both good times and difficult times solidified his confidence and knowledge of the Lord as the One who sustains him. When crisis hits we, like David, find that the Lord is the One sustains us during those times. David learned that when he called out to the Lord, the Lord answered him! This is so important – to know that the Lord hears and answers us – and that gives us confidence to cry out to the Lord for all that we need and to trust Him to sustain us, even in crisis when the stakes seem much higher.

The Lord took David on a journey throughout his life so that he got to the place where he "...did not fear though tens of thousands assail me on every side." (Psalm 3:6). Amazing! David is describing a time of great crisis in his life, yet even in that time he did not fear. Our prayer is that we would all be able to make this same declaration during the various crises in our lives. The only way we learn these lessons is through developing our relationship with the Lord over time, learning to hear and obey His voice, and learning to receive all we need from Him – He truly is the One who sustains!

1.) Do you know the Lord as your help and as the One who sustains you? Do you, like David, know that when you call out to the Lord that He answers you? Reflect and write some of the ways the Lord has heard and answered your prayers.

_____
_____
_____

2.) What about the situations in your life where you had difficulties and could not take care of them on your own? Did the Lord show up in that place of need? Recount the testimony of God's faithfulness and His power to sustain you.

_____
_____
_____

3.) How does it make you feel when you hear David say that tens of thousands assailed him on every side, yet he did not fear? Would that be your response today? Ask the Lord to reveal your fears to you. Write what He says here.

_____
_____
_____

Ask Him to help you release your fears to Him, specifically as you consider your preparedness journey and the crises that are sure to come.

_____
_____
_____

Come Away With Me
Read Mark 6:30-31

1.) During crisis there is so much going on and so much to do. People naturally have greater needs than usual as they now find themselves in a situation that is unfamiliar. As one who will lead in crisis, there will be lots of amazing stories, difficult decisions, and like the disciples, much to tell. How do you deal with people with great needs? How do you maintain your level of peace when the barometer of activity and stress is rising?

_____

_____

_____

2.) In Mark 6:31 it tells how the disciples were so busy they did not even have time to eat. When you get stressed or very busy, is your natural tendency to eat or to skip meals? What other coping mechanisms do you use when experiencing high stress? What is a more healthy strategy to deal with high stress?

_____

_____

_____

3.) The Lord's solution is this, "Come away with me by yourself to a quiet place and get some rest." Maintaining this quiet place of rest and refreshment with the Lord is essential, in our daily life, but especially in disaster. Does your life look different on the days or weeks that you get more time with Jesus? What about when you get little time with Jesus, how does this affect your life, power, and light output?

_____

_____

_____

— Session Four —
Day Five Prayer Topic

Pray for _____

Spend this time praying for the situation your class has decided upon. Continue to ask God to speak to you about specific people or details in this situation. He loves to reveal His heart for those in distress. Ask Him what's on His heart today.

_____

_____

_____

_____

SAFE HOME &
GRAB AND GO BAGS
SESSION FIVE

NOTES

_____

_____

_____

_____

_____

_____

_____

_____

_____

_____

_____

_____

_____

_____

_____

SAFE HOME & GRAB AND GO BAGS

1.) The Safe Home Assessment is meant to assess the capacity, threat, and _____ of your home.

2.) Presenting an appearance of _____ is as important as security itself.

3.) Regarding security you are only as strong as your _____ link. A solid steel door does little good with a large bay window right next to it.

4.) It is important to evaluate and realize your _____ so that you know to what extent you may extend hospitality.

5.) Bottom Line of Safe Home – GET _____: inventory supplies, know your capacity, and have an intentional plan.

6.) When do we GO?! Evacuation is a _____ decision!

7.) Four reasons to evacuate your home include lack of pure _____, and physical, chemical, and _____ threats.

SESSION 5 SUMMARY

Your safe home is only as strong as your weakest link. This session will teach you to assess your home's capacity, threat, and vulnerability. Capacity is the number of people you can sustain and care for in times of crisis. Vulnerability refers to the areas of your home that are not as secure as they could be. The appearance and allusion of security is as important as security itself. Your home is your strong physical fortress – know it as well as you know your strong fortress in the Lord.

SAFE HOME ASSESSMENT

Using the Safe Home Assessment Checklist, have your family, or maybe even a friend, take a tour to evaluate all facets of your home. We encourage bringing the family and a friend, because others may see weaknesses and strengths that you would miss. Become aware of everything around you – trees, electrical lines, gas lines, position on your street, details of perimeter, open access points, etc.

Scott's Safe Home Assessment Checklist

PHYSICAL HOME	ILLUSION OF SECURITY	PHYSICAL PLAN
❑ Keep doors and windows locked	❑ Keep mail picked up	❑ Evacuation Plan – written, shared, and practiced
❑ Upgrade locks and strike plates by screwing into studs	❑ Car in the driveway	❑ Practice intruder de-escalation on each other
❑ Lighting and motion lights	❑ Keep all entries lit	❑ Ask yourself and others the tough questions
❑ Use an alarm system	❑ Keep big boots on the porch next to the dog dish	❑ How far do I take security?
❑ Plywood windows (storms)	❑ Signage: Beware of Dog and Security Alarm signs	❑ Plan alternate means of defense
❑ Landscape awareness	❑ Fake cameras (they sell them)	❑ Get training if necessary

A consistent weakness found in many homes are ground floor or large panel windows. Several companies like 3M make window security films for residential installation. Although they are expensive they do offer benefits such as: crime prevention by impeding quick entry through windowpanes and glass doors and severe weather and accident protection by helping hold panes in place to minimize flying glass.

After having done an exterior assessment of your home, there are many preparations to be made on the inside. The first of which is creating a safe room that provides protection from airborne threats, gas spills, and possible intruders. This room should have a possible evacuation route and as few windows as possible so you can seal out airborne threats. You may have an additional safe room specifically for storms. This room should be towards the center of your house and, best case scenario, have no windows.

SAFE ROOM OR SHELTER-IN-PLACE

This designated place of protection from environmental threat is called a safe room or shelter-in-place. This room needs to be equipped with tape and plastic for sealing off the windows and a towel to place in front of the crack under the door. An airborne threat will usually dissipate in five to eight hours unless it is a burning source (fuel tanker wrecked on nearby highway). It is good to have activities for children, a portable toilet option (unless your safe room includes a bathroom), food and water, grab and go bags are nice to have, and a crank radio so you'll know when you can come out.

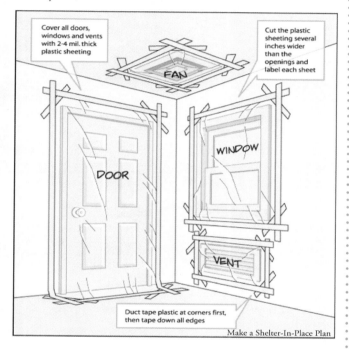

Cover all doors, windows and vents with 2-4 mil. thick plastic sheeting

Cut the plastic sheeting several inches wider than the openings and label each sheet

FAN

DOOR

WINDOW

VENT

Duct tape plastic at corners first, then tape down all edges

Make a Shelter-In-Place Plan

And yes, if you have sealed off your safe room really well, there is a chance that you could run out of oxygen eventually. Asphyxiation is a more serious threat than the risk outdoors. If you notice someone has a rapid pulse rate and shallow breath you need to get this person to a place where there is more oxygen.

SHELTER-IN-PLACE SUPPLIES

- Home Emergency Kit which includes food, water, first aid kit, additional supplies

- Duct tape, scissors

- Plastic sheeting to cover and seal doors, windows, air conditioners, ventilation systems

KNOW YOUR CAPACITY

This brings us back to capacity and enforces your need to **plan** for the number of people you can have in your home. **You must assess capacity before hospitality.** Even in the midst of a power outage, if your family is only prepared for three days and another family joins you during the event, you just cut your food and water duration in half. You will **have to say no** at some point. For longer-term disasters, you can deplete your resources and put people into **more** danger by allowing them in when you do not have the capacity to serve them.

Regardless of where you are on the Prep Step process, you must inventory your supply so that you know how much you have, how many it will serve, and for how long. This is the definition of capacity.

1 Year

WHAT'S YOUR ACTUAL FOOD CAPACITY?

3 Months

45 Days

22 Days

1 Person   4 People   8 People   16 People

We are preparing so that we may serve others. We know that there will be plenty of people with need, however, you have to rely on the Lord to speak to you, lead you, and protect your family too. Especially when your plan includes your family – children, grandchildren – does saying yes to someone else put those you have committed to serve in danger? You must have very clear boundary lines. When you let too many people in or give away too much, your primary responsibility is compromised. When you give away too much water too soon, the implications can be very serious. When you do tell someone no to a request for help, give them an alternative resource to find what they need, for example, "there is a gas station down the street and a food pantry on 36th Street."

Should you decide to serve food or give out water, do not do so from your own home. Someone who knows where the source is can create a dangerous situation when people get desperate.

SANITATION

Sanitation is a significant part of the capacity equation. If you overtax your sanitation system when services are down, the basement floods, the air is contaminated – you nullify your safe home, causing everyone to have to evacuate. Know your capacity. For more extended crises, you should make a plan for the removal of garbage (as not to attract rodents) and human waste (for health reasons). Be sure to store plenty of toilet paper, wipes (for children or babies), instant hand sanitizer, disinfectant, feminine supplies, baby needs (diapers, ointments), other personal hygiene supplies, garbage bags, and portable toilets. *See article titled More on Sanitation in the Appendix section for additional information.*

WE RECOMMEND:

Port-A-Potty with Five Gallon Bucket
Bolands.ThriveLife.com

SELF CARE

Taking care of yourself is what will afford you the ability to lead, care for, and serve someone else. You need to stay hydrated, eat three meals a day, sleep a sufficient amount of hours for your body, and drink Living Water – **do not compromise your time with the Lord during crisis**. Keep your spirit engaged with the Lord: worship, pray, read the Bible, and surround yourself with those who do the same. Schedule time with the Lord – you need to hear His voice and respond. This provides good leadership for those around you. Your team will also help you to make decisions that promote self care. We need each other – this is why we do not do it alone. Preparedness Peace is about preventing *you* from becoming part of the crisis.

FIRST AID

Another important issue to consider is first aid. Because many emergency response services can be overwhelmed and slow to respond, it is important that you have the ability to care for wounds and other first aid issues on your own. Here are two examples of recommended kits with basic and advanced supply lists. You may purchase already assembled kits or assemble your own.

The bottom line is that you must get organized, inventory your supplies, know your capacity, have an intentional plan, and maintain your safe home.

WE RECOMMEND kits from www.ZebGear.com (Referral code: prepstep)

BASIC KIT	ADVANCED KIT

BASIC KIT

1 - First Aid Instructions
1 - Burn Aid Package
16 Bandage Strips,1"x3"
1 - Tape Roll, Adhesive
5 - Butterfly Strips
1 - EMT Shears
1 - 4" Elastic Bandage
1 - Pair of Stainless Steel Tweezers
6 - Sterile Sponges, 4"x4"
2 - Ammonia Inhalants
1 - Blood Stopper Kit
6 - Antiseptic BZK Wipes
1 - Abdominal Pad, 5"x9"
6 - Safety Pins
1 - Triangular Bandage
1 - Pair Latex Examination Gloves
4 - Pain Relievers
1 - Three Compartment Bag

ADVANCED KIT

1 - First Aid Instructions
1 - 16 oz. Skin Flushing Solution
2 - Tongue Depressor
1 - Hand Soap
1 - Bandage Gauze, 3"x 4 yards
1 - 6" Elastic Bandage
4 - 4"x4" Sterile Sponges
2 - Bandage, 7"x 8"
4 - Abdominal Pad, 5"x9"
1 - Eye Pad
1 - Triangular Bandage, 40"x 40"x 56"
16 3" Bandage Strip
2 - Ice Pack
1 - EMT Shears
1 - 5" SS Hemostat
1 - Tweezers
2 - Sutures
6 - Safety Pins
2 - Pair Latex Gloves
10 Pain Reliever
1 - Pill Bottle
1 - Irrigation Syringe
2 - First Aid Cream
2 - Triple Antibiotic
1 - Burn Aid Package
2 - 1" Tape
15 Alcohol Wipes
15 Iodine Wipes
15 Antiseptic Wipes
15 Clean Wipes
1 - SAM / Universal Splint
1 - Lip Treatment
1 - Airway
1 - Field Dressing 11 sq. inch
1 - 3 Section Bag

WE RECOMMEND:

BlastMatch Fire Starter
Thrive Life
www.Bolands.ThriveLife.com

GRAB AND GO BAGS

Emergency evacuation can be necessary in minutes. A Grab and Go Bag is a portable kit that contains the items one would require to survive for 72 hours when evacuating from a disaster. The only thing you absolutely need in this emergency kit is drinking water since you can go without food for three days. But, the goal is to remain safe, healthy, and functioning for these three days, not just alive. The focus is on having what you need for evacuation, rather than long-term survival.

Organizations responsible for disaster relief and management estimate that it can take them up to 72 hours to reach people affected by a disaster and offer help, which is why we recommend that your grab and go bag contains supplies for up to 72 hours. Oftentimes, the bag is put to good use without leaving home. The bag's contents may vary according to the region where you live. Someone evacuating from the path of a hurricane may have different supplies than someone that lives in an area prone to tornadoes or wildfires.

We recommend that you prioritize the items that you will pack according to the following categories: **Fire:** for warmth and cooking; **Water:** filter/purify; **Shelter:** stay dry; **Food:** 2,000-3,000 calories per day. Additional significant considerations to make while packing your grab and go bag are physical strength, special needs (medications, baby/elderly/pet items), environmental conditions, and anticipated length of travel. Remember, you might be carrying this bag for a really long distance. Make sure you can do it. Limit the weight of the pack to 25 pounds maximum. A good way to distribute weight is by sharing items, prioritizing family content between each pack, and even children can carry lightweight items in their packs.

Spend time this week putting together a grab and go bag that is mobile and full of essentials to help your family survive for up to 72 hours. You can purchase a pre-assembled kit from Thrive Life, www.Bolands. ThriveLife.com, and dozens of other companies. Some prefer to use the list and make one custom-fit bag for your family's needs. Find the Grab and Go Bag list in the Lists section of this workbook. Store your grab and go bag in a convenient place. Train all family members that it is only for emergencies and discuss the contents with older children. Put all grab and go bag items in airtight plastic bags. Replace water, batteries, food, outgrown clothes, and medicine every six months or each time you change the clocks – medicine sooner if necessary.

In the event you are forced to evacuate your home and you have no plans or supplies in place, one of the only choices that will remain is to take your family to a public shelter. Plan ahead and get prepared so you will not have to do this. Again, our first recommendation is to stay and we strongly advise that you do not execute any type of evacuation without detailed, practiced plans. Regardless of your decision to stay or go, *well laid plans* are necessary to establish a safe home and to effectively use grab and go bags in case of evacuation. Walk in Preparedness Peace.

EVACUATION

Leaving your home and going somewhere else is a major decision! It is important that you have *solid* reasons to leave your house and all the preparations that you have made. You need to have a *plan* about what factors would cause you to leave your safe fortress. This will help reduce confusion and stress during crisis. **There are reasons to evacuate and they hinge on your physical safety being in danger – lack of water, chemical spill or threats, shelter is compromised, flood, fire, and civil unrest.** In leaving, you need to consider the possibility that your short-term evacuation could turn long-term. **The Holy Spirit *will* lead you.**

This is when the Memorandum of Understanding (MOU) is activated. A MOU means you have an agreement with a third party that in the event of disaster, you can evacuate to that location. When you evacuate, you could be going by car, on foot (keep a pair of good shoes in car), or by any other means you have for mobility (ATV or bicycle – these will help you to be able to carry more than when walking). If it is an automobile evacuation, you will be glad that your car is ready to go. Your gas tank should never fall below half full, the car kit emergency supplies will be in place, maps and routes chosen and practiced. Whenever possible use the routes you have planned because if others are looking for you, at least they will know routes you plan to travel and might be able to find you. The documents you've collected and copied will become very important in the event of an evacuation!

EVACUATION PLANNING GUIDELINES

Emergency Contact List and Phone Numbers
Include police, fire, doctor, hospital, schools, electric, gas, and water companies; place this list next to a phone in the home as well as in emergency grab and go bags.

Family Meeting Place
Should your family need to evacuate your home for any emergency, designate a nearby place to meet. Consider a neighbor's house or the nearest corner to your home. Also, it is a good idea to decide on a second location to meet that is away from your home in case you are not able to meet at the first location.

Plan Escape Routes
Plan a couple of different escape routes out of the home and out of town in the event you need to evacuate and your normal routes are blocked. Make sure the children understand and practice evacuating the home via the emergency exit routes: i.e. fire escapes, windows, etc.

Family Identification Photos
Make sure everyone in the family has a copy of a current photo of each family member that clearly shows their features in case you need to use these photos for family identification and searching efforts.

Important Documents to be Copied for Grab and Go Bags and Other Safekeeping
Photocopies of drivers license, passport, Social Security card, birth certificate, medical records, insurance policies and agent's phone numbers, and credit and identification cards, should be made for each member of your home. (Refer to the Comprehensive List of Suggested Documents to Copy found in Session 2.) Originals should be stored in your fire safe while copies of all of the above should be kept in your grab and go bags, and stored in a waterproof container/pouch. You may also feel comfortable with a trusted extended family member having a copy of this information as well.

Map of Local Area
Make sure you have a map of the local area and evacuation routes or places where you might go if evacuating and store them in a waterproof container.

Family Contact Information/Notification Network
Friends and relatives can be a part of your notification network. If you have members of your family living outside of your area or state, be sure and share this information with them and let them know your emergency notification plan to inform them of your family's status.

Notification Network Information
Each family member should carry this important information in their pack.

Contact Name _____
Address _____
Home Phone # _____
Cell Phone # _____
Email _____

Out of Area Contact Name _____
Address _____
Home Phone # _____
Cell Phone # _____
Email _____

Meeting place #1 _____
Phone Number or Description/Directions to Location
_____
_____
Meeting place #2 _____
Phone Number or Description/Directions to Location
_____

Additional Important Numbers
#1 _____
#2 _____
#3 _____

Share Information
Share the evacuation plans with your family *now* while it is still fresh. Email your extended family members and friends and inform them of your families' Notification Network Plan. Hard copies should be printed and stored in your grab and go bags in a waterproof container/pouch.

Also, send hard copies of the information above, including copies of the photos, to your extended and out of area family and friends.

Choose three or more of the questions below and share the answers in your group now.
*Recommended discussion questions

1.) What are the aspects of your home that immediately stand out as strengths or weaknesses of a safe home?

List them here: _____

_____

2.) What are ways you can "beef up" the appearance of security/occupancy in your home?

_____

_____

_____

3.) Rest is an essential part of maintaining a safe home. How will you rest and spend time with the Lord in a disaster situation?

Ideas: _____

_____

4.)* Regarding staying or going, what is your first instinct right now – do you think you would want your family to stay or go?

❏ We would choose to stay   ❏ We would choose to go

What situations might cause you to choose to go? _____

_____

5.)* Using the Grab and Go Bag list provided in the Lists section, what percentage of these items do you already have in your home? _____

Again, it's okay to get excited about gear; there are so many choices and so much cool stuff once you get into it!

There are _____ number of grab and go bags to prepare for my family.

6.) Name four physical threats and four chemical threats that would cause you to evacuate your home.

Physical threats: _____,_____,_____,_____,

Chemical threats: _____,_____,_____,_____.

PEACE | Biblical Focus and Discussion

Preview and discuss the verses to be studied during the week. Read each scripture aloud as a group and discuss first impressions, any current or past revelation on that verse, and pray together that God would speak to you as you study His Scripture this week.

SESSION FIVE | DAY ONE

Jeremiah 32:25 "And though the city will be handed over to the Babylonians, you, O Sovereign LORD, say to me, 'Buy the field with silver and have the transaction witnessed.'"

SESSION FIVE | DAY TWO

Jeremiah 32:17 "Ah, Sovereign Lord, you have made the heavens and the earth by your great power and outstretched arm. Nothing is too hard for you."

SESSION FIVE | DAY THREE

Jeremiah 32:42 "As I have brought all this great calamity on this people, so I will give them all the prosperity I have promised them."

SESSION FIVE | DAY FOUR

Isaiah 55:8-9 "For my thoughts are not your thoughts, neither are your ways my ways, declares the LORD. As the heavens are higher than the earth, so are my ways higher than your ways and my thoughts than your thoughts."

SESSION FIVE | DAY FIVE

Prayer Focus: _____

Share with your group what God is highlighting to you about this topic in your prayer time.

YouTube: History Channel, After Armageddon, Session 9

Websites: www.ZebGear.com (Referral code: prepstep)
www.adventuremedicalkits.com

Book: *Intimate Friendship with God: Through Understanding the Fear of the Lord* by Joy Dawson

Challenge: Watch this video http://youtu.be/TLtrntXifkY and take "Evacuation: The 10 Minute Challenge." Review your home evacuation plans and then put them into practice. Complete this challenge before the start of Session 6.

(Think how great it will feel to have all of this prepared!!)

1.) Do a Safe Home Assessment on your own home, and when appropriate, invite other members of the family – possibly even friends for an outsider's perspective – to join you on your assessment tour. Find Scott's Safe Home Assessment Checklist in this session.

❏ I have competed my Safe Home Assessment

2.) Locate the utility shutoffs at your home: gas ,water, electric.

I have located the ❏ gas shutoff ❏ water shutoff ❏ electrical panel box

3.) Strengthen two of the weaknesses you found during your Safe Home Assessment. For example, it could be as simple as adding a Beware of Dog sign or fixing the broken latch on the fence. It is up to you where you begin reinforcing your boundaries.

I/We chose to reinforce: _____

4.) **Family Plans and Documents:** This week, use maps to create your families' evacuation routes, including three to four alternate routes out of your city in different directions. Give maps or copies of routes to all who will evacuate with you. Make sure your Memorandums of Understanding (MOUs) are in place and that they understand the plans that you have made and the role they play in the plans.

Indicate here when you have:
❏ Created evacuation routes   ❏ Made or bought maps   ❏ Distributed maps
❏ Created MOUs and communicated with evacuation locations

5.) Assemble grab and go bags for each person in your family. Use the Grab and Go Bag list provided and remember the cost and the quality are determined by your personal preferences. Get the essentials packed – fire, water, food, and shelter. Keeping it simple is a good way to start, you can always *build* on this foundation.

❏ I assembled ____ (number) of complete grab and go bag(s).
❏ I need more time to finish this task.

6.) A number of people know that you are prepared; who do you think will show up at your house unannounced? How will you react to this? At what point will you say no to helping them?

❏ I have considered these possibilities. My capacity is _____ people.

7.) Read and respond to this session's daily devotionals on the following pages.

Chapter 32 of Jeremiah is all about obeying the voice of the Lord even when it doesn't make sense to our rational mind. As it says in Isaiah 55, the Lord's ways are not our ways, nor His thoughts our thoughts. We must *trust* the Lord when He speaks to us. Timing and rational sense become irrelevant when the Lord speaks. Obedience is *key*. May we have the insight, faith, comfort, and trust in the Lord that Jeremiah demonstrates as he walks faithfully before the Lord.

Trust and Obey
Read Jeremiah 32:6-12

At the beginning of Chapter 32, Jeremiah is imprisoned for prophesying to Zedekiah – king of Judah – that Jerusalem would be handed over to the king of Babylon. The Lord specifies that if Zedekiah tries to fight against the Babylonians that he would not succeed. As a matter of fact, "...by sword, famine and plague [Jerusalem] will be handed over the king of Babylon...". Jeremiah 32:36.

Meanwhile, the Lord says to Jeremiah in verse 7, "Your uncle is going to come to you and say, 'Buy my field at Anathoth, because as nearest relative it is your right and duty to buy it'" and just as the Lord said, it happened. In verse 8 and 9 Jeremiah says, "I knew that this was the word of the Lord, so I bought the field at Anathoth..."

1.) Jeremiah is convinced the city of Jerusalem will be destroyed and handed over to the king of Babylon. Yet he hears the Lord instruct him to invest in the land and he obeys. This does *not* make sense to the rational mind. Have you ever heard or felt the Lord leading you to do something that didn't make sense? Did you do it? It's always worth it! Describe your experience.

_____
_____
_____

2.) Talk and pray with your buddy about your strengths and weaknesses regarding hearing the Lord's voice and obeying. Specifically ask the Lord how to encourage this person and then tell them what He said.

Notes for your buddy:_____
_____

What did your buddy say about you? _____
_____

Ask your buddy to hold you accountable for obeying the Lord even in the small things and even when it doesn't make sense.

3.) What is the most bold decision you have made in obedience to the Lord? How did it turn out? What did you learn about God and yourself in the process?

_____
_____
_____

4.) This session's homework is to evaluate your safe home and finalize your evacuation plans. But when disaster strikes and it is time to make decisions for your family, remember Jeremiah. Remember that if the Lord speaks to you, **obey** Him and trust that He sees and knows **much** more than you. Spend time now thanking the Lord for His leadership in your life. Pray today for faith to rise up in your heart. Ask God to prepare you now for the mighty things He will do as you **lean** on Him in the places of need that will arise.

_____

_____

— Session Five —
Day Two Devotional

Trust and Obey
Read Jeremiah 32:13-25

In this passage the Lord is giving very practical, specific instructions to Jeremiah about how to protect the deed for a long time. The Lord knows that this act of obedience will prove to be very fruitful for Jeremiah in the future. We know that Jeremiah believes the Lord, but as he prays, beginning in verse 17, he reminds himself that "nothing is too hard for [God]." In his prayer he fixes his eyes on **who** God is, praises God as he recites all the mighty works he has witnessed personally and also those he has heard about for generations. In verse 23 he processes with the Lord what he sees happening around him and then closes his prayer with clear understanding of what the Lord said about Jerusalem and what the Lord said for him to do.

1.) There is a very literal application from the text to the process of documentation you have completed in this course. Our security is not found in our property or the things that we own, but stewarding well all that we have received. This matters to God. How does it feel to have all of our documentation in order and protected?

_____

_____

2.) In the middle of a trial, have you ever reminded yourself of specific instances from the past of the faithfulness and kindness of the Lord towards you or towards others? What did this do for your spirit/heart/attitude? This is an important focus to cultivate.

_____

_____

3.) It is important that we recognize the power of focusing on **who God is** in the midst of crisis. When Job had been stripped of everything he loved and had worked so hard to build – his family, his health, his livestock – God Himself "answered Job out of the storm" (Job 38:1) and **comforted** him by reminding Job **who He is** – even in the midst of crisis. If this is how God comforted Job, then we should comfort others in this same way. Why would reminding people **who God is** comfort them in the midst of crisis?

_____

_____

4.) When we know who God is, it is easier to _____.

Trust and Obey
Read Jeremiah 32:26-44

This passage is rather intense. In verse 27 the Lord starts out by asking Jeremiah the question, "Is anything too hard for me?" He states again that He will hand Jerusalem over to the Babylonians, and then He begins to explain why. Verse 33 sums it up nicely, "They turned their backs to me and not their faces; though I taught them again and again, they would not listen or respond to discipline." So He says they will be handed over by the sword, famine, and plague but goes on to say in verse 42, "As I have brought all this great calamity on this people, so I will give them all the prosperity I have promised them."

1.) Take verse 27 alone: "I am the Lord, the God of all mankind. Is anything too hard for me?" and proclaim it over a situation in your life that seems impossible. Strengthen yourself in the Lord. ***Remind*** yourself who God is and ***give*** Him this situation.

_____

_____

_____

2.) This passage is rich with promises from the Lord. Even in His discipline when the Lord is provoking His people, His heart toward them is ***good***. He sees the end from the beginning and knows the fruit this trial will produce in them. What specific promises did God make towards His people in this passage?

_____

_____

3.) How do you feel about God in this passage? Do you believe that God still disciplines His children today? In Hebrews 12:6, the author says, "...the Lord disciplines those he loves, and he punishes everyone he accepts as a son." What about nations? Would God ever bring destruction ***and*** redemption to a city? These are ***tough*** questions that can only be answered through personal revelation as you seek the Lord. These are also questions that those in crisis will be asking. Write your initial thoughts now and continue to seek the Lord about these things.

_____

_____

_____

_____

My Ways Are Higher Than Your Ways
Read Isaiah 55:8-11

1.) Think of a time of personal hardship or crisis. What did you come to know about the Lord during that time that you didn't know before?

_____
_____
_____

2.) What do you think the Lord is saying in verses 8 and 9? "For my thoughts are not your thoughts, neither are your ways my ways, declares the Lord. As the heavens are higher than the earth so are my ways higher than your ways and my thoughts than your thoughts." How does this make you feel?

_____
_____
_____

3.) Have there been times in your life when you've been able to trust God when what He was saying didn't make sense? Did you continue to trust Him when you couldn't see how the situation would turn out? As we continue on our journey and build a history of trusting God and allowing His ways to prevail in our lives, it will get easier and easier to trust Him in all circumstances. Ask the Lord to help you to agree with His ways and trust Him more and more.

_____
_____

4.) Anyone who has ever grown a garden understands how essential and powerful rain is to growth and fruit. The rain nourishes seedlings, causes them to grow and yield seed, which then can be used to make bread and feed a city. Verse 11 states God's Word is like this. Like the rain, it ***will*** cause things to bud and flourish in our lives and other peoples' lives. This should cause us to take great hope in the gospel of Jesus Christ, in the words He has spoken over our lives, and every promise whispered to our hearts. How does this verse impact your heart?

_____
_____
_____

Session Five
Day Five Prayer Topic

Pray for _____

Ask God to speak to you about specific people or details in this situation. Have you seen the Lord provide answers to your prayer?

_____
_____
_____

HOME SECURITY

SESSION SIX

89

NOTES

_____

_____

_____

_____

_____

_____

_____

_____

_____

_____

_____

_____

_____

_____

_____

_____

_____

HOME SECURITY

1.) Security is _____ from danger, risk, fear, anxiety, and doubt.

2.) It is important to build out _____ aspect of security, rather than relying on one source of security; i.e. a full pantry, the best grab and go bag, etc.

3.) You can create a strong _____ of security by using signage and props such as: Beware of Dog signs, security alarm signs, men's boots sitting outside on the porch, or fake cameras.

4.) Effective security comes from careful _____, clear communication, execution, and training.

5.) When dealing with a threat, your job is to de-escalate the situation with a confident and _____ voice. Remember, you need to *practice* this.

6.) Over 50 percent of robberies are due to an _____ door.

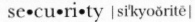

Dictionary Thesaurus   🔍 security ✕

se•cu•ri•ty |siˈkyoŏritē|

noun (pl. **-ties**)

1 the state of being free from danger or threat : *the system is designed to provide maximum* **security against** *toxic spills* | *job security.*

• the safety of a state or organization against criminal activity such as terrorism, theft, or espionage : *a matter of national security.*

• procedures followed or measures taken to ensure such safety : *amid tight security the presidents met in the Colombian resort.*

• the state of feeling safe, stable, and free from fear or anxiety : *this man could give the emotional security she needed.*

Oxford American Dictionary

Security is **not** a closet full of guns and ammunition nor is it a pantry full of food. Relying on one element of preparation alone will never give you security. Many people, when truly contemplating the things that could happen in crisis, wrestle with anxiety, doubt, and fear. Establishing a good security plan will bring freedom from these things. **A solid, well-rounded, plan that includes good communication, planned strategies, and lines of defense, locked doors, appearance of security, evacuation plans, training, and a prepared spirit will give confidence to individuals and teams**. Build out every aspect of security to achieve this well-founded confidence. As you are making plans for security, unity in this decision-making process is essential. Effective security comes from careful planning and clear communication. **Ultimate security is found in listening to the Lord, obeying what He says, and standing on His Word and promises for our life.**

Another reason it is so important to have a plan is because of the YOYO factor. Living in a You're On Your Own situation could occur for many reasons — severe weather, communication problems that prohibit you from calling for help, and due to overwhelmed or limited emergency response resources.

The best reaction to a threat is to have a plan in place. The *appearance* of security – things like men's boots, signage, fake cameras – and the confident show of strength will dissuade intruders from choosing your home. Scripted verbal defense is also very effective for people who approach the door. An intruder will not go into a situation they think is bigger than themselves.

However, in the event that an unknown person – a possible intruder – has approached your front door, the verbal strategies will operate to de-escalate the situation and send the person away. You must plan and train everyone in the home what to do in a situation like this and practice often. Do not think you can just implement it when you need it. Plan what you will do and say. Your strategy needs to include strong and clear communication to the person outside the door, time to assess the situation, communication with others in the house, and the ability to contact 911 if necessary and possible.

Addressing the person on other side of the door with a strong tone, confidence, and a directive voice indicates that you are in control of the situation. Ask clearly who they are and what they want, assess again, and tell them exactly what they need to do. As you portray a sense of security and strength, the person will know they are messing with the wrong home. These lines must be scripted and practiced until they can be implemented with confidence.

The following is a line that many people choose to use as a verbal strategy: "We are willing and able to defend ourselves if you enter. Please **go away** or we cannot guarantee your safety."

In the event that the person does not heed your warning and go away, we would recommend that you leave the front door, turn off all lights inside, and retreat with everyone in the house to the safe room. By your assessment and according to your plan, you need to determine if you should evacuate the house taking your grab and go bags or stay put and defend your property. Ask the Holy Spirit to help you make this important decision.

Should you choose to stay and defend your property, alternative forms of defense include a baseball bat, pepper spray, wasp spray, a stun gun, and mace. The use of these forms of defense also require a plan of evacuation. These sprays will only provide momentary protection. You must have a plan to get away immediately if you choose to use them.

The last line of defense includes a firearm. If you and your team decide that your security plan includes firearms then you must also plan to get everyone **trained** in safety, proper use, and respect for firearms. This is no small decision. Unity about every decision in security is essential to the health of a family or team in times of crisis.

The King of Kings is ultimately the only *real* and *sure* security we have. There is nothing more important than knowing that *only* the Lord can give us true security. Meditate on the Scriptures to the right as you consider that your security is in Him alone.

EXAMPLE HOME EVACUATION PLAN

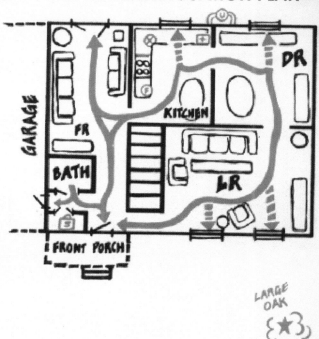

Psalm 118:6 "The LORD is for me; I will not fear; What can man do to me?" NASB

Psalm 56:11 "In God I have put my trust, I shall not be afraid. What can man do to me?" NASB

Philippians 4:6-7 "Be anxious for nothing, but in everything by prayer and supplication with thanksgiving let your requests be made known to God. And the peace of God, which surpasses all comprehension, will guard your hearts and your minds in Christ Jesus." NASB

Psalm 91:11 "For He will give His Angels charge concerning you, To guard you in all your ways." NASB

PEACE Small Group Interaction

Choose three or more of the questions below and share the answers in your group now.
*Recommended discussion questions

1.)* Take a look at each definition of security in the Summary section. Discuss with your group what security is and what it is *not*.

_____

_____

_____

2.) After discussing the definitions of security, to what level will you take your personal defense? Who are you accountable to in decisions such as these? Who will you consult regarding the decisions you make about security and why?

_____

_____

_____

_____

3.) How can you create security in the hearts and minds of your family?

_____

_____

_____

_____

4.)* Our true security is found in Christ. What does this mean to you? How do you achieve this? Do you really believe this?

_____

_____

_____

_____

5.) What was your response to the Intruder Response Demonstration?

_____

_____

6.)* As a group, it would be great to *practice* out loud (right now) what you would say to an unwanted guest or intruder. Take time and think about the words you would use. Find a partner and **say these words out loud** like you mean it!

_____

_____

_____

Seek the Lord about the security that is found in Him alone. Our prayer is for you to hear His voice about the plans to secure you home. We encourage you to ask the Lord for strategy to help others get prepared.

SESSION SIX | DAY ONE

Isaiah 26:3 "You will keep in perfect peace him whose mind is steadfast, because he trusts in you."

SESSION SIX | DAY TWO

Matthew 19:27-29 "Peter answered him, 'We have left everything to follow you! What then will there be for us?' Jesus said to them, 'I tell you the truth, at the renewal of all things, when the Son of Man sits on his glorious throne, you who have followed me will also sit on twelve thrones, judging the twelve tribes of Israel. And everyone who has left houses or brothers or sisters or father or mother or children or fields for my sake will receive a hundred times as much and will inherit eternal life.'"

SESSION SIX | DAY THREE

2 Kings 6:15-16 "When the servant of the man of God got up and went out early the next morning, an army with horses and chariots had surrounded the city. 'Oh, my lord, what shall we do?' the servant asked. 'Don't be afraid,' the prophet answered. 'Those who are with us are more than those who are with them.'"

SESSION SIX | DAY FOUR

2 Kings 6:17 "And Elisha prayed, 'O LORD, open his eyes so he may see.' Then the LORD opened the servant's eyes, and he looked and saw the hills full of horses and chariots of fire all around Elisha."

SESSION SIX | DAY FIVE

Prayer Focus: _____

Share with your group what God is highlighting to you about this topic in your prayer time.

Resources: Review Appendix for great resources

Websites: www.survivalblog.com

Book recommendation for women: *One Thousand Gifts* by Ann Voskamp

Scripture: Psalm 118

Challenge 1: Go camping for at least one night and use all of your preparedness gear.

Challenge 2: Lead your own Preparedness Peace group.

1.) ***Talk*** with your family about security. ***Pray*** with your family about security. Make a plan together – get everyone in your home ***on board*** with your security plan. You must be in agreement. Not having a plan will create division during a crisis.

Write out your security plan: _____

_____

_____

_____

❏ **I have prayed over and talked with my family about our security plan.**

2.) Devise a de-escalation plan. Have everyone in your home learn and practice verbal strategies to keep unwanted guests/intruders away from your home. Be sure that your children know what to do if you are not home in case any serious situations arise.

Write out your intruder de-escalation plan: _____

_____

_____

_____

❏ **My family has practiced the intruder de-escalation plan.**

3.) Gather supplies needed to shelter-in-place and prepare the room that will serve as your safe room. Include items and activities for children, a toilet solution, and evacuation goods.

❏ **We have our shelter-in-place supplies and have chosen and prepared our safe room.**

4.) Get others prepared. Meet your neighbors, collect and distribute ready.gov information as a tool, gather a group, help to build your community in a preparedness mindset, and share the love of Jesus as often as possible.

5.) Consider leading the Neighborhood Edition of Preparedness Peace as an outreach to co-workers and neighbors. This version contains the nuts and bolts of preparedness but puts the responsibility of sharing the gospel on you, the facilitator. To request information, go to www.PreparednessPeace.com and click 'Contact Us'.

6.) Get training in your areas of interest: first aid, Community Emergency Response Teams (CERT), Critical Incident Stress Management (CISM), in sharing the Gospel with others, self-defense, and Disaster Response Training. Consider a physical fitness plan. Your physical health is very important in keeping yourself and family safe.

7.) Read and respond to this session's daily devotionals on the following pages.

True Peace Comes from the Lord
Read Isaiah 26:1-16

This entire chapter is written in the context of disaster. However, even in the midst of great disaster, we see hope in the Lord and His promises – we see people clinging to and trusting in the Lord. Verse 3 promises that those whose mind is stayed on the Lord will be kept in perfect peace, even in the midst of incredibly trying times. The Lord is the only One who can keep us in perfect peace, but we must trust in Him! Verse 12 repeats the promise of the Lord being the One who establishes our peace. We see in verse 16 that in a time of crisis (whether it is individual crisis or of a more corporate nature), men will seek the Lord and pray to Him. We've probably all seen the truth of this in our own life or we know someone who chose to turn to the Lord during a crisis in their life.

1.) Verse 3 promises the Lord will keep us in perfect peace as we trust in Him. Do you believe that? Do you run to the Lord to receive His peace in trying times? Practice going to Him when difficulties arise in your life. Doing so will build that muscle in you for when the real crises come and develop a habit of going to the Lord. What current situation in your life could benefit now from the peace of the Lord?

_____

_____

_____

2.) Think about the security plans that you are making for your home. Can you imagine actually having to **use** them? **These** are the times we need to trust God and to maintain peace. Much easier said than done. How do you cultivate this?

_____

_____

_____

3.) Think about the many crises coming on the earth and the people who will be seeking God in the midst of them. What will you tell the ones seeking the Lord when that time comes? What tools have you developed so that you are able to minister to others in the midst of a crisis? Ask the Lord what ministry training and opportunities you should take advantage of in the coming months in order to be prepared to minister in the future.

_____

_____

_____

4.) Think about next steps in your preparedness journey. Does the fact that you know that crisis is coming and that people will seek the Lord motivate you to prepare others? Why or why not? Ask the Lord what your preparedness focus should be for the next six months: going further in your prep steps, preparing others, or both?

_____

_____

_____

The Glorious Reward
Read Matthew 4:18-20; Matthew 19:27-29

Peter and the other disciples are examples of those who trusted the Lord when He called them to follow Him. The Lord did not explain to them at that time what He was calling them to, but instead, just called them and expected them to follow. I love the response of these two brothers in Matthew 4:20, "At once they left their nets and followed him." One day, Peter finally asks Jesus the question that I believe was burning on his heart since he left to follow Jesus. Matthew 19:27, "We have left everything to follow you! What then will there be for us?" He was probably astounded by the answer. I believe these promises, given to them as a result of their trust and obedience, were way beyond what they ever imagined. The things that Peter and the other disciples gave up in order to follow Jesus pale in comparison to what they will receive as a result of their trust and obedience. This is also true of each one of us as we trust and follow Him.

1.) In Matthew 19:27 Peter finally asks Jesus a question that has probably been on his heart since the day he followed Him – in my paraphrase – what will be the result of our trust in You? At first I was surprised that Peter waited so long to ask Jesus this question, but I believe the delay was because Peter was walking – according to the promise of Isaiah 26:3 – in perfect peace because he had put his trust in the Lord. In your past when you chose to put your trust in the Lord and follow Him, has your heart been at peace? Ask the Lord to increase your peace today in an area you are not walking in it.

_____

_____

_____

2.) Is it difficult or scary for you to trust the Lord with your life and the life of your family? Think about situations where you chose to trust the Lord and how faithful He has been to you. Commit to trust and follow Him as you continue in preparedness, knowing the result will be more than you thought or imagined.

_____

_____

_____

3.) Each time you decide to trust the Lord do you think about promises the Lord has for you in the future as a result of trusting Him? Name the things you are trusting Him with now and anticipate the reward that will assuredly be given you.

_____

_____

_____

Leading in Crisis
Read 2 Kings 6:8-16

Again, we find ourselves in the middle of crisis and there is a man of God, Elisha, who knows things by the Spirit of God and is used by God to lead in crisis.

1.) Think upon verse 12 "...Elisha, the prophet who is in Israel, tells the king of Israel the very words you speak in your bedroom." Elisha, this man of God, is ***tuned*** in to the Spirit. We can see from this story that Elisha has many spiritual gifts and uses them to honor the Lord. What gifts has the Lord given to you? How do you use them to bring Him glory?

_____

_____

_____

2.) Elisha, called the man of God, is advisor to the king of Israel. Joseph was the wisest and most discerning man according to Genesis 41:39, in whom was the spirit of God, and he served as advisor to the king. Again, Scripture is revealing the need for men and women of God who know the Lord's voice and His heart to be ready to serve the leaders of our land in times of crisis. Whether on a family level or a national level, how is the Lord preparing you to ***lead*** others?

_____

_____

_____

3.) The principles of Proverbs 27:12 are at work in this passage. The king of Israel ***heeds*** Elisha's warnings and takes precautions as he travels. As this course comes to a close, do you feel there is any wise counsel the Lord is saying to heed? Do you feel you have any wise counsel for others?

_____

_____

_____

4.) In verses 15 and 16, Elisha's servant goes outside in the morning and is frightened to see an army surrounding their city! He yells, "Elisha! What should we do?" Elisha says, "Don't be afraid, those who are with us are more than those who are with them." This is the reason we do not walk this journey of faith alone. We ***need*** people who stand beside us and remind us of the truth. Are you surrounded by people who encourage you and speak truth over you? Seek out these friendships. Be this kind of friend and you will ***have*** these friends.

_____

_____

_____

Supernatural Protection
Read 2 Kings 6:15-23

1.) Elisha is a man who knows God. His trust in God **guards** his heart and mind. He walks in peace, has confidence in His ability to hear the Lord's voice, and pours himself into the lives of others. What do you think his personal life with the Lord looks like on a daily basis? How do you get to such a place of rest, wisdom, confidence, and discernment?

_____

_____

_____

2.) Talk about supernatural protection, look again at verse 17! The servant was not able to **see** the angels of the Lord that were there on behalf of Elisha, but this does not change the fact that they were there. When we are talking about security and crisis and YOYO, we must acknowledge the **truth**. We are **never** alone. The Lord is with us and He commands His angels concerning us. Furthermore, like Elisha, we have a heavenly army dispatched on our behalf in times of need. Research this in the Word, ask the Lord to reveal to you His nearness and provision – always – but especially in times of crisis.

_____

_____

3.) When Elisha's servant gets scared because he sees this army surrounding the city, Elisha **knows** that the forces of heaven are with him and he prays that his servant's eyes would be open to see the same. The **truth** is stated in Psalm 91:11, "For he will command his angels concerning you to guard you in all your ways." God had opened Elisha's eyes to see what was happening in the Spirit realm. When Elisha asked God, He opened the eyes of the servant as well. This is our role in the body of Christ – to help others see the truth and to pass on to others all we have received from the Lord.

4.) In verse 18, we see another example of supernatural protection. Elisha asked the Lord to move on his behalf and God **did** it. The Lord struck the army with blindness. In verses 19-23 Elisha leads them to the king, serves them a feast and loves his enemy – the men that came to capture him. The bands from Aram never raided Israel's territory again.

Wow! There is so much in this passage. Take time and write everything that stands out to you about supernatural protection and Elisha's leadership, decision making, and relationship with the Lord.

_____

_____

_____

_____

_____

Pray for _____

*Spend this time praying for the situation your class has decided upon. Ask God to speak to you about specific people or details in this situation. What moves your heart as you pray? Do you find yourself praying in a more specific direction? Stick with this and ask the Lord to reveal **more** to you today.*

_____

_____

_____

_____

_____

_____

APPENDIX

THE TRUTH ABOUT YOUR LOCAL GROCERY STORE

By James Wesley, Rawles on November 30, 2010 reprinted with permission from www.survivalblog.com

I've been reading your Blog for a little over a year now and find it very interesting. Not long ago there was an entry about trying to convince your family about the need to get prepared. I to have the same issue when trying to get others on board. They always seem to give me the "RCA dog look" – like I've lost my mind.

However, I do have the advantage of some work experience that helps. I've worked for a major grocer / big box retailer for the last 25 years. In that time things have changed an unbelievable amount. Twenty or even ten years ago we stored tons of merchandise in the back room and restocked throughout the day. Now due to the wishes of Wall Street all retailers are required to very closely monitor their inventory levels. If you want your share price to go up then you had to greatly reduce the amount of inventory you kept in the stores. This resulted in the Just in Time (JIT) inventory craze. Basically this means that instead of a store employee knowing what sold when and ordering each day/week to keep the store stocked with what was selling or what they knew would sell based on their experience it is now done by computers. Now this "computer" knows how long it takes to get each item from the vendor to the store. Then it takes information from the registers each day based on how much of an item is sold and/or sales trends and orders just enough as not to run out. The goal is that as a customer is buying the last item off the shelf that a stocker is coming down the aisle with a new case to restock.

Of course any of you who do any shopping understand this is not a perfect science. As people go shopping now they take for granted that what they want will be on the shelf. Most of the time this process does work as planned. When you consider that most stores carry 70,000 plus items there is a very small percent that are actually out each day.

The problem occurs when some outside factors come into play. This can be as little as the weather man predicting a snow or ice store. If that happens people go nuts buying everything they can get their hands on. The system is not set up for this. If the situation only affects a few locations then they can get back in stock within 2-3 days on most of the basic supplies. However if it affects a large region such as half a state then the warehouses run out fast also. They are on the JIT program as well and aren't stocked in a way to restock 100 stores all at once. Many areas of the country are primed to be affected by an earthquake. If that were to happen the shelves would be cleaned out within hours and wouldn't be restocked for who knows how long. Even if the stores local area wasn't affected, most likely the roads between the store and the warehouses would have bridges that if not destroyed would certainly be shut down for a time in order for inspectors to clear them as safe before trucks were allowed to cross.

The other factor I explain to folks is that when they shop day in and day out it looks like a ton of merchandise on the shelf. For example a store may stock 60 propane bottles for camp stoves on a regular basis. But in an emergency situation whether it has happened or only predicted the customers who get there first to buy some don't just buy one or two. They will buy at least 10 so then only the first six customers get any. Many of the big box and grocery stores you shop in every day average between 3,000 and 6,000 customers a day. Do the math.

As far as food most stores get 2-to-5 trucks a day of some type of food. Thus the store you shop at each day/week really only has about 1-½ to 2 days worth of food on the shelf any given day during normal conditions. If an emergency happens they will be cleaned out in a matter of hours. Then the question becomes how they will restock. Remember roads may be closed. The warehouse workers who normally load the trucks may have situations where they don't show up to work due to taking care of their own family. The same would be true with the truck drivers who would bring it to the stores and the folks who stock and run the local store as well.

What I try to make people understand it that they need to have a stock of what they need at their own house or somewhere. That they can't just assume the local store will have what they want. A lot of discussion goes on about food but you can't just think about food. Of course that is important for sure but also think about other things you would want. Such items might be batteries, candles, matches, charcoal, lighter fluid, Coleman fuel, propane, lamp oil, water carriers, and toilet paper (very important), etc. I also try to keep at least an extra 6-to-8 of such items such as toothpaste, soap, shampoo, paper plates, paper towels, medicine, etc. Think of things that you use every day but won't be able to drive to the store and pick up in the event of major crisis.

Assuming that you could buy gas or kerosene how many cans to you have to transport it in? A couple of years ago there was a major ice storm where I live. The stores were closed for 2-3 days in most cases. When they did open you couldn't find a gas can for days. Due to the storm everyone needed to run chain saws to clear roads, yards, or trees off their house. However like I said earlier the stores only replenish to rate of sale. Since a store doesn't normally sell 100 gas cans a day they don't keep that many in stock. Some items that became major needs but were not available that no one ever thinks about were two cycle oil and bar and chain oil for the chain saws, extra chains, files for sharpening, etc.

Another thing to consider is how you will pay of things if you can actually find them. Many times I've seen where some construction company digging a trench 100 miles away cut a fiber optic line and totally shut down all credit / debit card transactions and many check purchases. How much cash do you have on hand to buy things in an emergency? Be sure you don't keep $100 bills. Keep small bills and maybe some quarters. Even if the stores are able to stay open or reopen after a few days chances are they won't be able to get their change orders from the bank as they normally do 5-6

days a week. Thus if you walk in there with big bills they may not be able to make change.

The next time you go shopping take time to look around and think about what you would do if when you walked in the shelves were empty. What would you feed your family when you got home if you couldn't buy what you came to get. Go home and look at your cabinets. How long could you feed your family if you couldn't get to the store?

Many of you go shopping the day after Thanksgiving for the challenge of getting what you want to give for Christmas presents. Many of you won't go anywhere near a store that day because of the chaos. However, think about if you had to fight crowds like that who were fighting for food to feed their kids vs. just presents. If you had a proper store of supplies that you needed already you would certainly rest better knowing you didn't have to go and 'fight' in this dangerous environment.

I've said all this to simply say don't take for granted that what you run to the store for will always be there in a crisis. Make plans now and stock up on the basis as you see fit for your family. Remember to watch the sale ads and take advantage when stores run the items you use on sale. Also this holiday season is a great time to stock up on basic grocery items. Many stores have marked down items to attract customers for their holiday cooking needs. For example many stores have basic cans goods (beans, corn, etc) for 30-50% off their regular prices.

There are tons of list out there of what you need to have. Be sure to think about what you already use all the time and stock up on that as well. Life will be much more pleasant if live changes due to a major situation or even a temporary situation such as an earthquake if you don't have to drastically modify your life. Simple things like having your regular shampoo, soap, toothpaste, etc will be appreciated.

TOP 100 ITEMS TO DISAPPEAR FIRST DURING A NATIONAL EMERGENCY

July 27, 2007 Reprinted with permission from www.baconreport.blogspot.com

PREPAREDNESS PEACE DISCLAIMER: WE DO NOT RECOMMEND THIS BLOG BUT THIS LIST IS HELPFUL AND INTERESTING.

1. Generators (Good ones cost dearly. Gas storage, risky. Noisy... target of thieves; maintenance etc.)
2. Water Filters, Purifiers
3. Portable Toilets
4. Seasoned Firewood. Wood takes about 6 - 12 months to become dried, for home uses.
5. Lamp Oil, Wicks, Lamps (First Choice: Buy CLEAR oil. If scarce, stockpile ANY!)
6. Coleman Fuel. Impossible to stockpile too much.
7. Guns, Ammunition, Pepper Spray, Knives, Clubs, Bats & Slingshots
8. Hand can openers, hand egg beaters, whisks
9. Honey, syrups, white, brown sugar
10. Rice, beans, wheat
11. Vegetable oil for cooking. Without it food burns/ must be boiled etc.)
12. Charcoal, lighter fluid (Will become scarce suddenly)
13. Water containers (Urgent Item to obtain.) Any size. Small: HARD CLEAR PLASTIC ONLY– food grade if for drinking.
16. Propane cylinders (Definite shortages will occur)

17. Survival guide book
18. Mantles: Aladdin, Coleman, etc. (Without this item, longer-term lighting is difficult)
19. Baby Supplies: Diapers, formula, ointments, aspirin, etc.
20. Washboards, Mop Bucket with wringer (for laundry)
21. Cook Stoves (Propane, Coleman and Kerosene)
22. Vitamins
23. Propane Cylinder Handle-Holder (Urgent: Small canister use is dangerous without this item)
24. Feminine Hygiene, Haircare, Skin products
25. Thermal Underwear (Tops & Bottoms)
26. Bow saws, axes and hatchets, Wedges (also, honing oil)
27. Aluminum Foil Regular & Heavy Duty (Great Cooking and Barter Item)
28. Gasoline Containers (Plastic & Metal)
29. Garbage Bags (Impossible To Have Too Many)
30. Toilet Paper, Kleenex, Paper Towels
31. Milk – Powdered & Condensed (Shake Liquid every 3 to 4 months)
32. Garden Seeds (Non-Hybrid) (A MUST)
33. Clothespins, line, hangers (A MUST)
34. Coleman's Pump Repair Kit
35. Tuna Fish (in oil)
36. Fire Extinguishers (or large box of Baking Soda in every room)
37. First Aid Kits
38. Batteries (all sizes... buy furthest-out for Expiration Dates)
39. Garlic, spices, vinegar, baking supplies
40. Big Dogs (and plenty of dog food)
41. Flour, yeast, salt
42. Matches ("Strike Anywhere" preferred) Boxed, wooden matches will go first
43. Writing paper, pads, pencils, solar calculators
44. Insulated ice chests (good for keeping items from freezing in wintertime)
45. Heavy Duty Work Boots, belts, Levis, durable shirts
46. Flashlights, Lightsticks, torches, "No. 76 Dietz" Lanterns

46. Propane Cylinders (Definite shortages will occur)

47. Journals, Diaries, Scrapbooks (jot down ideas, feelings, experiences; Historic Times)

48. Garbage cans Plastic (great for storage, water, transporting – if with wheels)

49. Men's Hygiene: Shampoo, Toothbrush, toothpaste, mouthwash, floss, nail clippers, etc.

50. Cast iron cookware (sturdy, efficient)

51. Fishing supplies, tools

52. Mosquito coils, repellent, sprays, creams

53. Duct Tape

54. Tarps, stakes, twine, nails, rope, spikes

55. Candles

56. Laundry Detergent (liquid)

57. Backpacks, Duffel Bags

58. Garden tools and supplies

59. Scissors, fabrics, sewing supplies

60. Canned Fruits, Vegetables, Soups, stews, etc.

61. Bleach (plain, NOT scented: 4 to 6% sodium hypochlorite)

62. Canning supplies, (Jars, lids, wax)

63. Knives & Sharpening tools: files, stones, steel

64. Bicycles: Tires, tubes, pumps, chains, etc.

65. Sleeping Bags, blankets, pillows, mats

66. Carbon Monoxide Alarm (battery powered)

67. Board Games, Cards, Dice

68. d-Con Rat poison, MOUSE PRUFE II, Roach Killer

69. Mousetraps, ant traps, cockroach magnets

70. Paper plates, cups, utensils (stock up, folks)

71. Baby wipes, oils, waterless and Antibacterial soap (saves a lot of water)

72. Rain gear, rubberized boots, etc.

73. Shaving supplies (razors & creams, talc, aftershave)

74. Hand pumps, siphons (for water and for fuels)

75. Soysauce, vinegar, boullions, gravy, soup base

76. Reading glasses

77. Chocolate, Cocoa, Tang, Punch (water enhancers)

78. "Survival-in-a-Can"

79. Woolen clothing, scarves, earmuffs, mittens

80. Boy Scout Handbook, also Leaders Catalog

81. Roll-on Window Insulation Kit (MANCO)

82. Graham crackers, saltines, pretzels, trail mix, jerky

83. Popcorn, Peanut Butter, Nuts

84. Socks, Underwear, T-shirts, etc. (extras)

85. Lumber (all types)

86. Wagons, carts (for transport to and from)

87. Cots, Inflatable mattresses

88. Gloves: work, warming, gardening, etc.

89. Lantern Hangers

90. Screen Patches, glue, nails, screws, nuts and bolts

91. Tea

92. Coffee

93. Cigarettes

94. Wine, Liquors (for bribes, medicinal, etc.)

95. Paraffin wax

96. Glue, nails, nuts, bolts, screws, etc.

97. Chewing gum, candies

98. Atomizers (for cooling, bathing)

99. Hats, cotton neckerchiefs

100. Livestock

and for humor... here was a reply to the original post on The Bacon Report

"One thing you have left out is a lion costume. If you wear a lion costume you will terrify people into not taking your stuff. Also, small animals will drop dead from fright and you will be able to gobble them up. You may even meet a lioness, in which case you will be able to stay home while she goes out and catches the food. A lion costume should be Number One on your list."

FOOD STORAGE FOR $5 A WEEK

From: Olga Jones at www.outlands.tripod.com

[Olga says:]Know anyone who thinks they are too poor to prepare? Help is at hand, from the PREP list...

Okay I finally got the copies of the Food storage for $5 a week. I don't remember where I got it, but it wasn't off the internet. What you are supposed to do is set aside $5 a week and then buy specific items each week. You have a kitty set aside that you put the $5 in and you can't touch it for any reason but to buy the food storage item for that week. You put in whatever remaining change you have back into the kitty. Some things in the beginning are going to be cheap and then later will be more expensive. In order to pay for the expensive stuff later you need to keep the leftover money in the kitty.

Week 1:	2 cans tuna fish, 2 boxes salt
Week 2:	5 boxes of Macaroni and Cheese, 4 cans tomato soup
Week 3:	3 cans mushroom soup, 1 2.5 lb peanut butter
Week 4:	1 bottle vitamins
Week 5:	4 cans tomato soup, 1 10 lb powdered milk
Week 6:	1 bottle aspirin (500 tablets)
Week 7:	1 100 lb container wheat
Week 8:	1 5 lb powdered milk
Week 9:	1 5 lb honey
Week 10:	4 cans tuna, 4 boxes macaroni and cheese
Week 11:	1 10 lb sugar, 1 box salt
Week 12:	4 cans mushroom soup
Week 13:	1 bottle vitamins
Week 14:	1 100 lb wheat
Week 15:	1 box macaroni and cheese
Week 16:	1 5 lb honey
Week 17:	2 cans tuna, 4 can tomato soup
Week 18:	1 10 lbs sugar
Week 19:	1 100 lbs of wheat
Week 20:	2 10lbs of sugar
Week 21:	1 10lb powdered milk
Week 22:	1 can mushroom soup, 1 10 lb sugar
Week 23:	1 can tuna, 4 cans tomato soup, 1 10 lbs sugar
Week 24:	1 10 lbs sugar
Week 25:	2 cans tuna, 2 cans mushroom soup
Week 26:	1 100 lb wheat
Week 27:	3 10 lbs sugar
Week 28:	1 10 lb sugar
Week 29:	1 10 lb powdered milk
Week 30:	2 10 lb sugar
Week 31:	1 can tuna, 3 cans mushroom soup
Week 32:	1 can tuna, 4 cans tomato soup
Week 33:	1 100 lb wheat
Week 34:	2 cans tuna, 1 box salt
Week 35:	1 10 lb powdered milk
Week 36:	2 10 lb sugar
Week 37:	4 cans tomato soup, 2 boxes salt
Week 38:	Off week
Week 39:	1 100 lb wheat
Week 40:	1 10 lb powdered milk
Week 41:	3 10 lb sugar

Week 42:	2 cans tomato soup, 1 10 lb sugar
Week 43:	2 cans tomato soup, 2 cans mushroom soup
Week 44:	Off week
Week 45:	1 10 lb powdered milk
Week 46:	4 cans tomato soup, 4 cans mushroom soup
Week 47:	1 10 lb powdered milk
Week 48:	4 cans mushroom soup, 1 10 lb powdered milk
Week 49:	7 cans of tomato soup
Week 50:	7 cans of mushroom soup
Week 51:	2 10 lbs sugar, 1 box salt

A few weeks you will have "off" to replenish the kitty. I haven't figured it out myself, but by the end you should have 700lbs of wheat, 240 lbs sugar, 40 lbs of powdered milk, 13 lbs of salt, 10 lbs of honey, 5 lbs of peanut butter, 45 cans of tomato soup, 32 cans mushroom soup, 15 cans tuna fish, 10 macaroni and cheese dinners, 500 aspirin, and 730 multiple vitamins plus they suggest adding 6lbs of dried yeast and 6 lbs of shortening and this should be enough to sustain 2 people for a year. For every 2 people you have in your family add $5 more and double or triple the amount of whatever you are buying that week. I hope this makes sense and if you have any questions let me know. For those of you not in the US, you'll have to figure out the equivalents yourself, sorry.

Outlands Comments

You don't have 52 weeks. If you are just now starting and want to follow this plan, I seriously suggest you try to buy four "paper-weeks" every week. Don't forget this list is intended for just two people. Use this list, or any of the others on The Outlands, to go through your pantry and determine where you are *right now* and mark off what you already have. Then, take the list to the grocery store and spend $20 or so. Every week. Regularly. Print this list out and pass it around to others you know are starting to wonder about preparing a pantry.

MORE ON SANITATION

Waste disposal must be handled carefully in order to prevent disease, pests, and rodents. If sewer lines are not usable or if water is not available, there are a couple of options that could substitute for a functioning toilet.

1. Carefully place a garbage bag inside the toilet bowl. Use only for solids. Be careful that it doesn't puncture. Cover with lime or kitty litter to reduce odor.

2. Create a "bucket toilet" system. One idea is to use three buckets. The first has a regular toilet seat attached and is used only for solids. The second contains either lime, kitty litter, sawdust, or peat moss to cover the waste in the first bucket. The third bucket is used for urine. After the first bucket is full, the second bucket is used with the toilet seat, while contents of the first bucket are buried.

Important: To bury human waste, FEMA advised digging a pit two to three feet deep at least 50 feet downhill and away from any well, spring, or water supply. Other outdoor experts recommend 200 feet away from water sources. Urine isn't usually considered to be a problem and may be disposed of without a lot of concern about spreading disease.

To disinfect buckets, you may add one cup bleach to ½ gallon of water in the bottom. Some recommend sprinkling on baking soda, alcohol, laundry detergent, or Pine-Sol to control odor and germs.

3. You may also purchase a chemical toilet, porta-potty, or composting toilet.

4. In each of the above cases, biodegradable toilet paper is recommended.

Be sure to store plenty of toilet paper, wipes (for children or babies), instant hand sanitizer, disinfectant, feminine supplies, baby needs (diapers, ointments), other personal hygiene supplies, bleach, kitty litter or lime, garbage bags, and portable toilets.

TRASH

Get rid of clutter and dispose of things now, while trash service is dependable. Learn to re-use and recycle. Try to reduce and control the build up of trash in your home. When trash removal is disrupted: burn the burnables, if you can, in the fireplace or a campfire or in a barrel in the backyard. Use extreme caution because emergency response may be limited in case of fire. Non-burnables (like cans) should be compressed as much as possible and placed in trash bags inside trash cans with lids that can be clamped into place in order to prevent rodents and other animals from getting into it. Many food scraps may be composted by burying them in a trench along the edge of the garden. The exception would be bones, meat scraps, etc.

CONFIDENCE IN HIM

by Homer Owen at www.homerowen.com

"Do not be afraid of sudden terror, Nor of trouble from the wicked when it comes; For the Lord will be your confidence, And will keep your foot from being caught." Proverbs 3:25-26

If you will notice in the above verse these words - WICKED WHEN IT COMES. It does not say this with an IF in front of it. We all know that the wicked enemy does come and most of the time it comes with sudden terror. The Lord wants to encourage us that we can have absolute confidence in Him when the wicked comes. We serve a God that literally sits in heaven and laughs at the enemy when He sees him plotting against us.

"The kings of the earth set themselves, And the rulers take counsel together, Against the Lord and against His Anointed, saying 'Let us break their bonds in pieces and cast away their cords from us.' He who sits in the heavens shall laugh; The Lord shall hold them in derision." Psalms 2:2-4

We are told that the Lord will come and take us to His hiding place when the enemy comes in like a flood. Praise God that He will hide us in His dwelling place. One time I found myself on a wrong road in the Arab section of Israel of which I had been told to not go. I passed a car similar to the one I was driving that had been burned and less than a mile up the road I saw some Arabs standing in the road with machine guns. Yes, this was sudden terror and the enemy had come. I began to pray in the spirit and the Lord whispered in my ear that they were incapable of seeing me. What a joy it was to be able to pass right by them within inches and knowing that I was hid from their sight.

"You will show me the path of life; In Your presence is fullness of joy; At your right hand are pleasures forevermore." Psalm 16:11

Yes, He showed me the path of life that day and it was not to turn and run the other way but to continue down the road in full confidence that we greatly out numbered the enemy. Right on down the road the Lord directed my steps to take a turn and shortly there after I found myself on a marked highway that I traveled to my destination. I met a government official of Israel that morning and shared with him what had happened to cause me to be a little late for my appointment. He literally turned white and was amazed to know that I had made it safely to his office. He was surprised to see the abundant smile on my face. Praise God for the true joy of the Lord, which is our strength in time of trouble.

How wonderful it is to be able to go forth preaching the kingdom of God like Paul did. Praise God we are all servants of the most High God who refuses to take His eye off of us. Let us all purpose to stay in His mobile tent where His presence keeps us in complete confidence of His protecting hands.

"Then Paul dwelt two whole years in his own rented house, and received all who came to him, preaching the kingdom of God and teaching the things which concern the Lord Jesus Christ with all confidence, no one forbidding him." Acts 28:30-31

Continue to put your confidence in Him and rest in His loving-kindness for you.

ORIGINAL BLUE DAWN . . . IT'S NOT JUST FOR DISHES ANYMORE

From blog www.OneGoodThingByJillee.com

When you think about it....Dawn is a pretty amazing. It's great for washing dishes, pots and pans, flatware and crystal, but all the REST of the stuff it does is what makes it really extraordinary. It's ALMOST up there with Baking Soda as a versatile cleaning tool....almost.

Here is MY list of the "best of the best" ingenious uses for Original Blue Dawn gleaned from dozens of websites and reader's comments I have visited:

SAVING WILDLIFE
Ever wonder why Dawn Dishwashing Liquid is the wildlife cleaner of choice after an oil spill? According to the International Bird Rescue Research Center, Dawn effectively removes grease but does not cause harm to the skin of the birds. It's also biodegradable and contains no phosphates.

BUBBLES
According to Bubbles.org, Dawn dishwashing liquid makes great homemade bubbles. Here is the Giant Bubble Recipe used in bubble makers at many children's museums:

    1/2 cup Ultra Dawn
    1/2 gallon warm water
    1 tablespoon glycerin (available at any drug store)
    OR White Karo syrup works too!

Stir gently. Skim the foam off the top of the solution (too much foam breaks down the bubbles). Dip bubble wand and get ready for some good, clean fun!

GREASY HAIR PROBLEMS
Kids get into the darnedest things! Like Vaseline and baby oil rubbed into their hair! Dawn is mild enough to use on their hair and strong enough to remove the most stubborn grease.

HAIR PRODUCT BUILDUP
Once a month use original Dawn as you would shampoo. It will remove excess oil from your hair and scalp and strip away any build-up of styling products without any damage. Perform this once a month and you won't have to buy expensive salon products that do the same thing.

MANICURE SECRET
Soak fingers in full-strength blue Dawn. It makes the cuticles soft and easy to work with. And it removes the natural oil from the fingernails, which allows the polish to adhere very well.

REPEL HOUSEPLANT INSECTS
A safe, effective way to repel insects from your houseplants, including aphids, spider mites and mealy bugs. Put a drop of Dawn Dishwashing Liquid in a spray bottle, fill the rest of the bottle with water, shake well, and mist your household plants with the soapy water.

CLEAN YOUR WINDOWS
Try this recipe from Merry Maids: mix 3 drops Dawn in 1 gallon water and fill a spray bottle with the solution. Spritz and wipe as you would with any window cleaner.

PETS AND PESTS
Use it to bathe the dogs. It kills fleas on contact and is much cheaper than expensive dog shampoos.

CLEAN AUTOMOTIVE TOOLS
After you have finished your automotive repair project, soak your dirty tools in Dawn before you put them away to remove all the oil and grime. Dawn also helps prevent rust from forming on the tools.

ICE PACK

Partially fill a strong zip-type sandwich bag with Dawn dishwashing liquid, close and freeze. The liquid soap stays cold much longer and it can be re-frozen many times. It will conform to the place you need an ice pack.

TUB AND SHOWER CLEANER

Take a spray bottle and fill it halfway with white vinegar. Heat in the microwave. Fill the rest of the way with blue Dawn. Put lid on and shake to mix well. Spray on your tub and shower walls. Allow to sit for a few minutes and rinse away. It will totally melt all the gunk, slime, sludge and other stuff that builds up including a bathtub ring.

REPEL ANTS

Spray counter-tops, cupboards and any other area where you see ants with a solution of Dawn and water. Wipe dry. The slight residue of Dawn that remains will not be a problem at all for kids or pets, but ants hate it. Should you see a trail of ants, go ahead and hit them with the Dawn spray.

STRIPPING CLOTH DIAPERS

Add a squirt or two of original Dawn dish soap to your washer and run a hot wash, then rinse until there are no more bubbles. Dawn is a degreasing agent and helps stripping by removing oily residue. Be sure to rinse, rinse, rinse until the water runs clear.

UNCLOGGING TOILETS

A cup of Dawn detergent poured into a clogged toilet allowed to sit for 15 minutes and then followed with a bucket of hot water poured from waist height will clear out the toilet.

POISON IVY

Poison ivy spreads through the spread of the oil within the blisters. Washing the affected area with Dawn, especially on children who keep scratching the blister's open, helps dry up the fluid, AND keep it from spreading.

DRIVEWAY CLEANER

If you have gasoline or motor oil stains on your driveway, you can use the kitty litter method to clean up the excess oil and then use a scrub broom and a solution of biodegradable Dawn dishwashing detergent and warm water to safely and effectively remove excess motor oil from the pavement.

OILY SKIN

Dawn makes a great facial cleanser for oily skin. A drop or two combined with warm water will do the trick.

PAINT OR GREASE REMOVER FOR HANDS

Dawn combined with corn oil makes for the perfect paint or grease remover. Simply combine a little bit of both in your hands then rub it over affected areas. The corn oil and the dishwashing liquid both help to dissolve the grease and paint – yet leave skin soft, unlike harsher paint removers.

CLEANING THE KIDDIE POOL

Plastic wading pools can get very gunky, very fast. Dump the water, then scrub the pool with Dawn and a sponge. More potent cleaners like bleach will weaken and dry out the plastic in the sun.

MULTIPURPOSE CLEANER

Merry Maids recommends using a drop of Dawn in water to clean ceramic tile and no-wax/linoleum floors. You can also use the spray on:

- Bathroom and kitchen counters and sinks.
- Woodwork, e.g., baseboards, shelves, and wainscoting. (Dry as you go—wood doesn't like prolonged contact with water.)
- Tubs and toilet seats.

LAUNDRY PRE-TREATER FOR OILY STAINS

For oil-based stains such as lipstick, grease, butter, motor oil, cooking oil, and some pen inks, simply apply some Dawn dishwashing liquid directly to the stain and scrub with a small brush or toothbrush until the oil is removed, and then launder as usual.

NON-TOXIC LUBRICANT

Sliding glass doors, door knobs, hinges etc. It lasts much longer than any aerosol type spray that I have tried. And Its non-toxic! It does a great job of cleaning the parts that its lubricating as well!

SIDEWALK DE-ICER

For icy steps and sidewalks in freezing temperatures, mix 1 teaspoon of Dawn dishwashing liquid, 1 tablespoon of rubbing alcohol, and 1/2 gallon hot/warm water and pour over walkways. They won't refreeze. No more salt eating at the concrete in your sidewalks

POOL CLEANING

Squirt Dawn down the middle of the pool and all of the dirt, suntan lotion, etc. will move to the edges of the pool for easy clean up! AND it makes the pools sparkle.

EYEGLASS DEFOGGER

Simply rub a small drop of Dawn on eyeglass lenses, and wipe clean. It will leave a very thin film that will prevent them from fogging up.

SHOWER FLOORS

Cover greasy footprints on shower floors with a coating of Dawn; let sit overnight. Scrub away the gunk in the morning with a stiff brush.

APHID CONTROL ON FRUIT TREES

Mix two tablespoons Dawn to a gallon of water and put in your sprayer. Try to get spray both sides of the leaves, branches and the tree trunks. Let sit for about 15 minutes and then rinse the trees THOROUGHLY!

BIBLIOGRAPHY

"FEMA Declared Disasters by Year." ESL Power Systems, Inc. on the Web. Available online at http://www.eslpwr.com/manual-transfer-switch-preparedness.htm.

Hewitt, Mike, and Krassimir Petrov. "Money Supply and Purchasing Power." Dollar Daze on the Web. Available online at http://dollardaze.org/blog/?post_id=00583.

Kanalley, Craig. "U.S. Fault Lines GRAPHIC: Earthquake Hazard MAP." Huffington Post on the Web. Available online at http://www.huffingtonpost.com/2010/01/22/us-fault-lines-graphic-ea_n_432948.html.

"Make a Shelter-in-Place Plan." Federal Emergency Management Agency on the Web. Available online at http://www.ready.gov/business/plan/shelterplan.html.

Noy, Ilan. "The Macroeconomic Aftermath of the Earthquake/Tsunami in Japan." Econbrowser on the Web. Available online at http://www.econbrowser.com/archives/2011/03/guest_contribut_8.html.

Perlman, Howard. "The Water in You." USGS on the Web. Available online at http://ga.water.usgs.gov/edu/propertyyou.html.

Rice, Doyle. "More severe weather due after a brief lull." USA Today on the Web. Available online at http://www.usatoday.com/weather/storms/tornadoes/2011-05-08-tornadoes-floods-forecast_n.htm?csp=hf.

VIEWER GUIDE ANSWER KEY

SESSION 1
1.) happen
2.) fear
3.) confidence
4.) lifestyle
5.) team
6.) convenience
7.) urgency

SESSION 2
1.) Relationship
2.) resources, strength, support, safety
3.) responsible
4.) fail
5.) comfort

SESSION 3
1.) minutes, days, weeks
2.) 1 (one)
3.) without
4.) surface
5.) eight
6.) eat
7.) high, high
8.) 2,000- 3,000

SESSION 4
1.) planning
2.) location
3.) children
4.) YOYO
5.) doors
6.) throw

SESSION 5
1.) vulnerability
2.) security
3.) weakest
4.) capacity
5.) organized
6.) major
7.) water, environmental

SESSION 6
1.) freedom
2.) every
3.) appearance
4.) planning
5.) directive
6.) unlocked

LISTS

PREPAREDNESS RESOURCE BINDER

We recommend that you purchase a 3-ring binder and build a personal preparedness library. The binder is meant to serve as a resource to hold all important documents, articles, lists, strategies, and ideas that you come across in your preparedness journey. We have discussed the importance of *not* relying on the Internet in times of crisis. Use this binder to consolidate all necessary and desired crisis information.

We have already placed essential Lists in the Lists section of the workbook. These lists are mentioned all through the workbook and video. These lists will guide your shopping, packing, and procuring of emergency supplies.

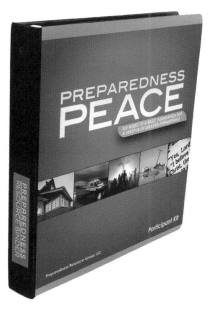

Your binder will be unique to your family, but here are some suggested organization tips to get you started. Get dividers and label each tab according to your priorities – suggested tab titles include:

- **Family Plans and Documents (all documents you determined to copy from the Comprehensive List of Suggested Documents to Copy, Evacuation plans, Emergency Contact Information, etc.)**
- **Food (purchase plans, recipes, storage, rotation details)**
- **Water (filtration and purification instructions, ways to harvest water, sources of fresh water)**
- **Medical (First Aid information/instruction, medication lists, natural remedies)**
- **Energy**
- **Security**
- **Communications**

Add documents you have copied, written, found online and want accessible to grab and go or reference in times you really need them. It is suggested that choice documents are placed in plastic page protectors to keep your documents clean and unwrinkled. Pockets may be helpful for larger documents.

The convenience and confidence of having all important documents and information in one place will be a great asset in times of crisis.

PREP STEP INVENTORY®

This list is meant to help you assess your current level of readiness, identify specific items to purchase, and track progress made towards your preparedness goal. This is a consolidated list highlighting items necessary in each category. On the checklist below, required items are marked with ○ **Have:** ○ **Need:** and include space for the quantity. The items not required in that category are marked by **N/A**.

There is always room for personal preference and the voice of the Lord to alter our suggestions. Remember, the Grab and Go Bag can supplement both the home and car kit.

ITEM	HOME	GRAB AND GO BAG	CAR
Certain items need to be packed per person in each category below. Do the math. Have enough for everyone in your family.	These items need to be assembled together in your home and designated for preparedness purposes. Make sure everyone knows where they are located.	The Grab and Go Bag can supplement both the Home Emergency Supplies and the Car Kit. We encourage you to prepare the bag, and then use where needed.	Car Kit can be supplemented with Grab & Go Bag, but in the event you only have what's in car, make sure items in car are sufficient.
WATER	2 gallons/person/day	As much as you can carry easily	Several gallons
Filtration/purification	○ Have: ○ Need:	○ Have: ○ Need:	○ Have: ○ Need:
FOOD			
2,000-3,000 Calories/day	○ Have: ○ Need:	○ Have: ○ Need:	○ Have: ○ Need:
Can opener	○ Have: ○ Need:	N/A	○ Have: ○ N/A
Eating utensils	○ Have: ○ Need:	○ Have: ○ Need:	○ Have: ○ N/A
Hand sanitizer	○ Have: ○ Need:	○ Have: ○ Need:	○ Have: ○ Need:
ENERGY			
Flashlights/headlamp	○ Have: ○ Need:	○ Have: ○ Need:	○ Have: ○ Need:
Batteries	○ Have: ○ Need:	○ Have: ○ Need:	○ Have: ○ Need:
Candles	○ Have: ○ Need:	○ Have: ○ Need:	N/A
Matches/lighter	○ Have: ○ Need:	○ Have: ○ Need:	N/A
Solar lamp/flashlight	○ Have: ○ Need:	N/A	○ Have: ○ Need:
Glow Sticks	N/A	○ Have: ○ Need:	N/A
Firewood	○ Have: ○ Need:	N/A	N/A
Solar/battery fans	○ Have: ○ Need:	N/A	N/A
Cooking stove	○ Have: ○ Need:	N/A	N/A
Generator	○ Have: ○ Need:	N/A	N/A
Fire extinguisher	○ Have: ○ Need:	N/A	○ Have: ○ Need:
MEDICAL			
Family first aid kit	○ Have: ○ Need:	○ Have: ○ Need:	○ Have: ○ Need:
Training: First aid CPR	○ Have: ○ Need:	N/A	N/A
COMMUNICATION			
Hand crank emergency radio	○ Have: ○ Need:	○ Have: ○ Need:	N/A
Emergency contact information	○ Have: ○ Need:	○ Have: ○ Need:	○ Have: ○ Need:
Solar charger	○ Have: ○ Need:	N/A	N/A
Phone/charger	○ Have: ○ Need:	N/A	○ Have: ○ Need:
FAMILY PLANS AND DOCUMENTS			
Maps/Evacuation Plans	○ Have: ○ Need:	○ Have: ○ Need:	○ Have: ○ Need:
Copies of all documents	○ Have: ○ Need:	○ Have: ○ Need:	N/A

continued on reverse...

ITEM	HOME		GRAB AND GO BAG	CAR
TOOLS/SUPPLIES				
Wrench	○ Have:	○ Need:	Multi Tool	Small Tool Kit
Pliers	○ Have:	○ Need:	N/A	N/A
Socket set	○ Have:	○ Need:	N/A	N/A
Black garbage bags	○ Have:	○ Need:	○ Have: ○ Need:	○ Have: ○ Need:
Duct tape	○ Have:	○ Need:	small roll	○ Have: ○ Need:
Basic hand tools	○ Have:	○ Need:	N/A	N/A
Crow bar	○ Have:	○ Need:	N/A	N/A
Sturdy tow rope	N/A		N/A	○ Have: ○ Need:
Jumper cables	N/A		N/A	○ Have: ○ Need:
Flat tire inflation canister	N/A		N/A	○ Have: ○ Need:
GPS	N/A		N/A	○ Have: ○ Need:
Spare tire, jack, wrench	N/A		○ Have: ○ Need:	○ Have: ○ Need:
Shovel/camping shovel	○ Have:	○ Need:	○ Have: ○ Need:	N/A
Hammer	○ Have:	○ Need:	N/A	N/A
Small box of nails	N/A		○ Have: ○ Need:	N/A
100 ft medium strength rope	N/A		N/A	○ Have: ○ Need:
Tarp	N/A		N/A	○ Have: ○ Need:
Dome tent	N/A		○ Have: ○ Need:	N/A
Compass	N/A		○ Have: ○ Need:	N/A
Notebook and pencil	N/A		○ Have: ○ Need:	N/A
Sewing Kit	N/A		○ Have: ○ Need:	N/A
Roadside flares	N/A		○ Have: ○ Need:	yes
Whistle	N/A		○ Have: ○ Need:	N/A
Extra set of keys	N/A		○ Have: ○ Need:	N/A
Cash	○ Have:	○ Need:	○ Have: ○ Need:	N/A
Ziplocs – large and small	N/A		○ Have: ○ Need:	N/A
50 ft Nylon Rope	N/A		○ Have: ○ Need:	N/A
Shleter-in-place supplies	○ Have:	○ Need:	N/A	N/A
PERSONAL				
Set of clothes	○ Have:	○ Need:	○ Have: ○ Need:	○ Have: ○ Need:
Poncho/umbrella	○ Have:	○ Need:	○ Have: ○ Need:	○ Have: ○ Need:
Sturdy shoes	N/A		○ Have: ○ Need:	○ Have: ○ Need:
Blankets	○ Have:	○ Need:	○ Have: ○ Need:	○ Have: ○ Need:
Gloves	N/A		○ Have: ○ Need:	○ Have: ○ Need:
Stocking hat	N/A		○ Have: ○ Need:	N/A
SPECIFIC NEEDS				
Feminine hygiene	○ Have:	○ Need:	○ Have: ○ Need:	○ Have: ○ Need:
Medication	○ Have:	○ Need:	○ Have: ○ Need:	N/A
Toilet paper	○ Have:	○ Need:	○ Have: ○ Need:	N/A
Soap, toothpaste, toothbrush	○ Have:	○ Need:	○ Have: ○ Need:	N/A
CHILDREN				
Entertainment/activities	○ Have:	○ Need:	○ Have: ○ Need:	N/A
Diapers/formula	○ Have:	○ Need:	○ Have: ○ Need:	N/A
Medicine	○ Have:	○ Need:	○ Have: ○ Need:	N/A
PETS				
Cage to transport	○ Have:	○ Need:	N/A	N/A

PERSONAL AWARENESS QUIZ:
EMOTIONAL AND SPIRITUAL CARE IN CRISIS

Self-Care Questions – Give prayerful consideration

We must be able to care for ourselves during crisis. If we cannot care for ourselves, our ability to care for others will be short-lived. Take this time to get to know yourself, your body, your emotional responses, and how you maintain your heart before the Lord and others. These questions deal with your personal responses and readiness for situations that could arise in the context of disaster. Read over these questions this week and in the future. *Answer the ones that you can and pray and ask others about the ones you don't know the answers to.* Many times others see things in us that we don't see in ourselves. Again, there is no end to the value of doing this as a team. Knowing yourself, how you respond, and what you need is very important as you work together with others.

I. In Advance of Crisis/Disaster – Become Aware of Me

A. What are my early warning signs of excessive stress? (anxiety, can't sleep, lose temper, overindulge, can't hear God, etc.)

B. How do I handle stress, both positively and negatively? (pray, worship, read the Bible, do deep breathing, exercise, eat ice cream, watch TV, ignore the signs, yell at my friends, eat chocolate!) *Communicate with your team/family how they can help you in this situation.*

C. What am I doing for self-care now – daily? Weekly?

D. What improvements do I need to make to my self-care plan? Who can I be accountable to as I implement these changes?

E. Have I realized how important it is in crisis to be physically fit, not only for my safety and comfort, but to better help others? Am I fit?

F. Am I spiritually ready? *Some ways to become more ready are: scripture memory, solid knowledge of the goodness and faithfulness of God, eyes fixed on Jesus no matter the cost, and a strong prayer life.*

G. What do I need in my "comfort kit?" (scriptures, pictures of family, favorite poem, music, favorite shirt, snack, etc.)

Take time to reflect and write your responses to some of the questions above.

_____
_____
_____
_____
_____

II. Physical/Practical

A. Am I ready to deal with the additional labor and time that is necessary when the power is out and modern conveniences are not available to me?

B. How can I prepare myself and my family for the living conditions in a disaster scenario? How many people do we plan to house with us and what will that be like for me and my family?

C. How much alone time do I need; how will I get it?

D. Is my body fit enough to evacuate by foot if necessary, carrying my pack and addressing needs of children and family?

E. How do I respond to limited choices for food, schedule, sleep, recreation?

F. How will I stay physically and mentally healthy? Do I need exercise, deep breathing, or naps? How am I with setting boundaries?

G. What are my indicators that I am stressed/need help? *Be sure to share these indicators with others so that they can help you take care of you.*

Take time to reflect and write your responses to some of the questions above.

_____
_____
_____
_____
_____

III. Emotional

A. Every crisis situation will be different and I have no way of knowing what may happen. How well do I handle the unknown? How do I need to prepare in advance to deal with the devastation me and my family may encounter?

B. Besides the physical devastation of the landscape, there may be enormous emotional and spiritual devastation – people who are in shock, angry, confused, belligerent, hopeless, or in need of medical or psychological care. How will I handle that? How do I care for them well? How do I deal with my own secondary trauma?

C. Am I ready to deal with my own "stuff" (weakness, brokenness) as it comes up during crisis? What strategies will I use to calm myself/rest/connect with God? How do I care for me- emotionally?

D. Have I dealt with my own inner healing issues from the past? Anything that has not been dealt with will get triggered in the rigors of extended crisis. Have I acknowledged areas of loss in my life and grieved well? Have I forgiven past injustices so I'm free of unforgiveness and bitterness? Am I grounded in the love of God and feel the Father's love for me? Do I draw strength from His delight over me? Do I really believe He is good?

Take time to reflect and write your responses to some of the questions above.

_____

_____

_____

_____

_____

_____

IV. Spiritual

A. Ultimately, it's all about people encountering God. Am I ready to give an answer to the hope that is within me, share my faith, and lead people in prayer for salvation? Can I do basic discipleship with someone?

B. How comfortable am I praying for people?

C. Am I ready to deal with the issue of God's discipline and mercy? Where am I in the process of wrestling with these issues in my own heart? Is my heart settled on the goodness, kindness, and faithfulness of God even in the midst of disaster?

D. How will I answer the question, "How can a good God let this happen?"

E. Do I realize that in the context of crisis, I may have the opportunity to minister the love and gospel of Jesus to each person I meet? What will I say?

Take time to reflect and write your responses to some of the questions above.

_____

_____

_____

_____

_____

_____

Ready
Prepare. Plan. Stay Informed.

Family Emergency Plan

Make sure your family has a plan in case of an emergency. Before an emergency happens, sit down together and decide how you will get in contact with each other, where you will go and what you will do in an emergency. Keep a copy of this plan in your emergency supply kit or another safe place where you can access it in the event of a disaster.

Out-of-Town Contact Name: _____ Phone: _____

Email: _____

Neighborhood Meeting Place: _____ Phone: _____

Out-of-Neighborhood Meeting Place: _____ Phone: _____

Out-of-Town Meeting Place: _____ Phone: _____

Fill out the following information for each family member and keep it up to date.

Name: _____ Social Security Number: _____
Date of Birth: _____ Important Medical Information: _____

Name: _____ Social Security Number: _____
Date of Birth: _____ Important Medical Information: _____

Name: _____ Social Security Number: _____
Date of Birth: _____ Important Medical Information: _____

Name: _____ Social Security Number: _____
Date of Birth: _____ Important Medical Information: _____

Name: _____ Social Security Number: _____
Date of Birth: _____ Important Medical Information: _____

Name: _____ Social Security Number: _____
Date of Birth: _____ Important Medical Information: _____

Write down where your family spends the most time: work, school and other places you frequent. Schools, daycare providers, workplaces and apartment buildings should all have site-specific emergency plans that you and your family need to know about.

Work Location One
Address:
Phone:
Evacuation Location:

School Location One
Address:
Phone:
Evacuation Location:

Work Location Two
Address:
Phone:
Evacuation Location:

School Location Two
Address:
Phone:
Evacuation Location:

Work Location Three
Address:
Phone:
Evacuation Location:

School Location Three
Address:
Phone:
Evacuation Location:

Other place you frequent
Address:
Phone:
Evacuation Location:

Other place you frequent
Address:
Phone:
Evacuation Location:

Important Information	Name	Telephone Number	Policy Number
Doctor(s):			
Other:			
Pharmacist:			
Medical Insurance:			
Homeowners/Rental Insurance:			
Veterinarian/Kennel (for pets):			

ADULT CARD

Family Emergency Plan

Personal ID

Name: _____ DOB: _____
Address 1: _____ State: _____ Zip: _____
Address 2: _____ State: _____ Zip: _____
Home Phone: _____ E-mail: _____
Cell Phone: _____ Other E-mail: _____

Special Needs, Medical Conditions, Allergies, Important Information:
_____
_____

Ready ✓

< FOLD HERE >

Work

Business Name: _____
Address: _____ State: _____ Zip: _____
Office Phone: _____
Point of Contact or Special Instructions: _____

Work Emergency Plan: _____
_____

< FOLD HERE >

Children

Name: _____ DOB: _____ Sex: _____
Identifying Characteristics: _____
School/Daycare: _____ Address: _____
School Phone: _____ Cell Phone: _____
Name: _____ DOB: _____ Sex: _____
Identifying Characteristics: _____
School/Daycare: _____ Address: _____
School Phone: _____ Cell Phone: _____
Name: _____ DOB: _____ Sex: _____
Identifying Characteristics: _____
School/Daycare: _____ Address: _____
School Phone: _____ Cell Phone: _____

< FOLD HERE >

Neighborhood Emergency Meeting Place

Name: _____
Address: _____ State: _____ Zip: _____ Phone: _____
Point of Contact or Special Instructions: _____

Out of Neighborhood Emergency Meeting Place

Name: _____
Address: _____ State: _____ Zip: _____ Phone: _____
Point of Contact or Special Instructions: _____

Out of Town Emergency Meeting Place

Name: _____
Address: _____ State: _____ Zip: _____ Phone: _____
Point of Contact or Special Instructions: _____

< FOLD HERE >

Important Numbers or Information

Name: _____ Phone: _____
Name: _____ Phone: _____
Name: _____ Phone: _____
Name: _____ Phone: _____
Name: _____ Phone: _____
Name: _____ Phone: _____
Name: _____ Phone: _____
Name: _____ Phone: _____

Pets

Name: _____ Type: _____ Age: _____
Name: _____ Type: _____ Age: _____
Veterinarian Phone: _____

DIAL 911 FOR EMERGENCIES

Family Emergency Plan

Personal ID

Name: _____ DOB: _____
Address 1: _____ State: _____ Zip: _____
Address 2: _____ State: _____ Zip: _____
Home Phone: _____ E-mail: _____
Cell Phone: _____ Other E-mail: _____

Special Needs, Medical Conditions, Allergies, Important Information:
_____
_____

Ready ✓

Work

Business Name: _____
Address: _____ State: _____ Zip: _____
Office Phone: _____
Point of Contact or Special Instructions: _____

Work Emergency Plan: _____
_____

Children

Name: _____ DOB: _____ Sex: _____
Identifying Characteristics: _____
School/Daycare: _____ Address: _____
School Phone: _____ Cell Phone: _____
Name: _____ DOB: _____ Sex: _____
Identifying Characteristics: _____
School/Daycare: _____ Address: _____
School Phone: _____ Cell Phone: _____
Name: _____ DOB: _____ Sex: _____
Identifying Characteristics: _____
School/Daycare: _____ Address: _____
School Phone: _____ Cell Phone: _____

Neighborhood Emergency Meeting Place

Name: _____
Address: _____ State: _____ Zip: _____ Phone: _____
Point of Contact or Special Instructions: _____

Out of Neighborhood Emergency Meeting Place

Name: _____
Address: _____ State: _____ Zip: _____ Phone: _____
Point of Contact or Special Instructions: _____

Out of Town Emergency Meeting Place

Name: _____
Address: _____ State: _____ Zip: _____ Phone: _____
Point of Contact or Special Instructions: _____

Important Numbers or Information

Name: _____ Phone: _____
Name: _____ Phone: _____
Name: _____ Phone: _____
Name: _____ Phone: _____
Name: _____ Phone: _____
Name: _____ Phone: _____
Name: _____ Phone: _____
Name: _____ Phone: _____

Pets

Name: _____ Type: _____ Age: _____
Name: _____ Type: _____ Age: _____
Veterinarian Phone: _____

DIAL 911 FOR EMERGENCIES

CHILD CARD

Family Emergency Plan

Personal ID

Name: ____ DOB: ____
Address 1: ____ State: ____ Zip: ____
Address 2: ____ State: ____ Zip: ____
Home Phone: ____ E-mail: ____
Cell Phone: ____ Other E-mail: ____

Special Needs, Medical Conditions, Allergies, Important Information:
____
____

Ready ✔

< FOLD HERE >

School / Daycare

School Name: ____
Address: ____ State: ____ Zip: ____
Office Phone: ____
Point of Contact or Special Instructions: ____

School Emergency Plan:
____
____
____

< FOLD HERE >

Parent / Guardian / Care Giver

Name: ____ Home Phone: ____
Address 1: ____ State: ____ Zip: ____
Address 2: ____ State: ____ Zip: ____
Work Phone: ____ E-mail: ____
Cell Phone: ____ Other E-mail: ____
Identifying Characteristics: ____

Name: ____ Home Phone: ____
Address 1: ____ State: ____ Zip: ____
Address 2: ____ State: ____ Zip: ____
Work Phone: ____ E-mail: ____
Cell Phone: ____ Other E-mail: ____
Identifying Characteristics: ____

< FOLD HERE >

Neighborhood Emergency Meeting Place

Name: ____
Address: ____ State: ____ Zip: ____ Phone: ____
Point of Contact or Special Instructions: ____

Out of Neighborhood Emergency Meeting Place

Name: ____
Address: ____ State: ____ Zip: ____ Phone: ____
Point of Contact or Special Instructions: ____

Out of Town Emergency Meeting Place

Name: ____
Address: ____ State: ____ Zip: ____ Phone: ____
Point of Contact or Special Instructions: ____

< FOLD HERE >

Important Numbers or Information

Name: ____ Phone: ____
Name: ____ Phone: ____
Name: ____ Phone: ____
Name: ____ Phone: ____
Name: ____ Phone: ____
Name: ____ Phone: ____
Name: ____ Phone: ____
Name: ____ Phone: ____

Name: ____ Type: ____ Age: ____ **Pets**
Name: ____ Type: ____ Age: ____
Veterinarian Phone: ____

DIAL 911 FOR EMERGENCIES

Family Emergency Plan

Personal ID

Name: ____ DOB: ____
Address 1: ____ State: ____ Zip: ____
Address 2: ____ State: ____ Zip: ____
Home Phone: ____ E-mail: ____
Cell Phone: ____ Other E-mail: ____

Special Needs, Medical Conditions, Allergies, Important Information:
____
____

Ready ✔

School / Daycare

School Name: ____
Address: ____ State: ____ Zip: ____
Office Phone: ____
Point of Contact or Special Instructions: ____

School Emergency Plan:
____
____
____

Parent / Guardian / Care Giver

Name: ____ Home Phone: ____
Address 1: ____ State: ____ Zip: ____
Address 2: ____ State: ____ Zip: ____
Work Phone: ____ E-mail: ____
Cell Phone: ____ Other E-mail: ____
Identifying Characteristics: ____

Name: ____ Home Phone: ____
Address 1: ____ State: ____ Zip: ____
Address 2: ____ State: ____ Zip: ____
Work Phone: ____ E-mail: ____
Cell Phone: ____ Other E-mail: ____
Identifying Characteristics: ____

Neighborhood Emergency Meeting Place

Name: ____
Address: ____ State: ____ Zip: ____ Phone: ____
Point of Contact or Special Instructions: ____

Out of Neighborhood Emergency Meeting Place

Name: ____
Address: ____ State: ____ Zip: ____ Phone: ____
Point of Contact or Special Instructions: ____

Out of Town Emergency Meeting Place

Name: ____
Address: ____ State: ____ Zip: ____ Phone: ____
Point of Contact or Special Instructions: ____

Important Numbers or Information

Name: ____ Phone: ____
Name: ____ Phone: ____
Name: ____ Phone: ____
Name: ____ Phone: ____
Name: ____ Phone: ____
Name: ____ Phone: ____
Name: ____ Phone: ____
Name: ____ Phone: ____

Name: ____ Type: ____ Age: ____ **Pets**
Name: ____ Type: ____ Age: ____
Veterinarian Phone: ____

DIAL 911 FOR EMERGENCIES

HOME EMERGENCY SUPPLIES

Below are the recommended items for a basic home emergency kit. Remember to plan water and food for each member of your family (including pets and others who you know will arrive in times of crisis). Most items you will have in your home already. Place these supplies in the designated preparedness area of your home. Start with the essentials and build from there.

WATER
Minimum three days supply of water per person
1 gallon per day for drinking
1 gallon per day for sanitation
Water purification tablets
Water filter

FOOD
**Minimum three days supply of food per person
(2,000-3,000 calories per day)**
Non-perishable food that requires no heating
(Freeze-dried, canned, air tight packaging)
Items like chili, soup, peanut butter, dried fruit
Can opener
Eating utensils

ENERGY
Flashlights/headlamp
Extra batteries
Candles, 100 hour candles
Matches (waterproof) and lighters
Solar-powered lights
In Winter: Plan heat source – firewood, tools to manage fire
In Summer: Battery-powered fans if no generator or solar power
Gas grill and extra propane bottles for cooking
Generator (if you choose)
Fire extinguisher – Remeber to keep close and ready

MEDICAL
High-quality first aid kit suitable for your family's needs and size
Take first aid and CPR training

COMMUNICATION
Hand crank or battery-powered weather or emergency radio
Emergency contact information
Phone, chargers, extra batteries, solar charger

TOOLS
Wrench
Pliers
Socket set
Black garbage bags
Duct tape
Basic hand tools
Crow bar
Shovel
Hammer
Scissors
Plastic sheeting

SPECIFIC NEEDS/PERSONAL HYGIENE
Feminine hygiene products
Toilet paper, paper towels, soap, towels, etc.
Toothbrush, toothpaste
Hand sanitizer
Medications

PERSONAL
Set of clothes
Umbrella/poncho
Blankets

CHILDREN
Entertainment items: activities, coloring books, games
Diapers
Formula
Medicine

PETS
Cage for transport
Food
Water
Medication and special needs

My Additional Items
_____
_____
_____
_____
_____
_____
_____

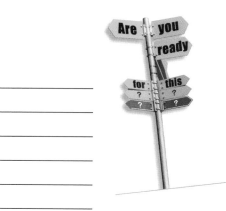

Car Emergency Supplies

These items could be very helpful if kept in the car that you would likely use in an evactuation but also could be useful in day to day road side emergencies. When coupled with your complete GRAB and GO bags you should find yourself adequately prepared to survive in your car should you become stranded or evacuating.

Water (Several gallons)

High energy power/food bars

Small tool kit

Jumper Cables

Flat tire inflation Canister (non-explosive)

Spare tire and jack

First aid supplies

Flash light and batteries

Non batteried flash light (solar)

Road side Flares

Maps/ GPS

Blankets

Umbrellas

First Aid kit

Sturdy Tow Rope

Gloves

Duct tape

Large plastic sheeting

Heavy duty garbage bag

Grab and Go Kit

If your emergency plan is to evacuate your home, you'll need a survival kit with essential gear and supplies to last at least 3 days (72 hours). The only thing you absolutely need in this emergency kit is drinking water since you can go without food for 3 days. But, the idea is to remain safe, healthy, and functioning for these three days, not just alive.

Spend some time putting together a 72 hour kit that is fairly easy to move and full of essentials to help your family survive. You can purchase a pre-made, convenient kit from dozens of different companies or use the list below to make one custom-fit for your family's needs.

Store your kit in a convenient place. Train all family members that it is only for emergencies and discuss with older children what it contains.

Put all kit items in airtight plastic bags. Replace water, batteries, food, medicine every six months - medicine sooner if necessary. Christmas and 4th of July are easy to remember dates. Also update outgrown clothes and other item needs at these times.

Items with a **PP** mean "Per Person"

- 1 large plastic tub with tight lid - store everything in it except water and blankets.
- 1 list of contents
- about 12 ZipLoc bags, 1 gallon size to hold items
- 1 blanket or sleeping bag PP - takes up a lot of space. Keep stored by emergency kit.
- **Water** - 2 gallons PP - 8lbs/gallon will make this the heaviest part of your kit. Consider keeping the water out of the kit and sitting right by it.
- **Food** - 4000 calories PP - food bars or other high-energy, ready-to-eat items. See emergency food supply for suggestions.
- **First Aid Kit** - have a family first aid kit sitting on your 72 hour emergency kit as well as a vehicle kit in each car and a personal kit in each family member's backpack or purse.
- **Tools**
    - 1 Plastic bowl, spoon, cup PP
    - 1 LED headlamp flashlight with extra batteries
    - 1 battery operated radio - receive emergency info
    - 1 multi-function camping knife
    - 1 small ABC fire extinguisher
    - 1 dome tent - backpacking tent sized for family
    - 1 each crescent wrench, hatchet, hammer, phillips and flat screwdrivers, pliers
    - 1 fold-up camping shovel
    - 1 Compass
    - 1 Local map and state map
    - 2 roadside signal flares
    - 1 notebook and pencil
    - 1 sewing kit, needles and thread
    - 1 medicine dropper
    - 1 whistle
    - 1 set of extra car and house keys
- **Supplies**
    - $100 cash
    - 1 roll duct tape

    - 1 roll plastic sheeting
    - 1 box waterproof matches
    - 1 roll aluminum foil
    - 4 ZipLoc bags, 1 gallon size PP
    - 2 large garbage bags PP
    - 4 disposable hand warmers PP
    - 2 candles
    - 2 snap light sticks
    - 1 small box of nails
    - 50 feet nylon rope
- **Sanitation**
    - 1/2 roll toilet paper PP
    - 4 alcohol towelettes PP
    - 1 small bottle liquid soap
    - Feminine supplies as needed
    - 1 toothbrush PP
    - 1 small bottle Purel hand sanitizer
    - 1 small bottle unscented chlorine bleach
- **Clothing**
    - 1 clothing change PP
    - 1 pair sturdy shoes PP
    - 1 emergency rain poncho PP
    - 1 hat and gloves PP
- **Specific Needs**
    - Infant Supplies - formula, bottles, powdered milk, baby food, diapers, ...
    - Elderly - medications, denture needs, hearing aid batteries, eye glasses, ...
    - Medical - insulin, prescriptions, supplies for contacts
- **Documents** - originals/copies in waterproof container
    - Wills, passports, social security cards, insurance policies, property deeds, contracts, stocks, immunization records, bank account numbers, credit card numbers, birth-marriage-death certificates, important phone numbers, inventory of household items

THREE WEEKS TO THREE MONTHS SUPPLIES

Car-Individual Backpacks Kept in Cars:
- Water bottles filled
- 1 crank flashlight
- Headlamp
- 4 flares
- 4 energy bars
- Small first aid kit
- Emergency reflective blanket or lightweight wool blanket
- Poncho
- Waterproof matches and butane lighter
- Multipurpose knife
- Fleece, hat, gloves
- Hand warmers
- Extra pair of tennis shoes that fits the driver
- Toilet paper
- Cash in $20s and small bills
- Reflectors
- Whistle
- Battery-powered radio
- Emergency light sticks
- Personal medication
- Personal sanitary supplies
- Wipes
- Warm socks
- Water purification tablets or water purifier. i.e. Katadyn camping water filters

Car-Carry in the Car:
- Gas with extra gas can
- Fix-a-Flat
- Tow rope
- Jumper cables
- Ice scraper
- Basic tools
- Shovel
- Extra fan belt, radiator hoses, fuses
- Cans of oil

Emergency Outdoor Shelter in Winter:
- Large tent with repair kit
- 25' x 60' plastic sheeting
- 10' x 12' plastic waterproof tarp
- 150' cording or rope
- Hammer
- Pocket knife
- Duct tape

Family Grab and Go Bin:
Note: Do everything you can to stay. Only leave if your life depends on it, you're being evacuated, or if you know you're going to a place that is out of the danger area i.e. relative or friend's house. It's MUCH MORE DANGEROUS out on the road with hundreds of others who don't have resources. Try to go in a caravan with others.

- Water: one gallon of water per person per day for drinking and sanitation
- Water purifier. Camping type single bottle Sawyer or Katadyn brand with extra filters. They start at $50 but you can put water in them from the most polluted river and drink right away.
- Food: 3-5 day supply per person of non-perishable ready to eat food.
- Hand crank radio and a NOAA Weather Radio with tone alert and extra batteries
- Crank flashlights (no batteries needed)
- Flashlights and extra batteries
- Whistle to signal for help or fog horn
- Dust mask, to help filter contaminated air
- Plastic sheeting/tarps
- Duct tape to shelter-in-place
- Moist wipes
- Garbage bags and plastic ties for sanitation
- Wrench or pliers to turn off utilities
- Manual can opener for food
- Maps
- Cell phone with charger
- Extra prescription medications (as much as you can get ahead of time)
- Prescription glasses (extra pair)
- Infant formula
- Diapers
- Pet food and extra water for your pet
- Important family documents in a waterproof, fireproof portable safe
  - Copies of insurance policies
  - Credit card numbers and phone numbers
  - List of relative's numbers
  - Birth certificates
  - Passports
  - Bank account records
  - Cash
  - Cash and change

- 1 Sleeping bag or bedding for each person
- Extra pillows and blankets for other refugees
- Bleach: Plain chlorine bleach, medicine dropper. When diluted nine parts water to one part bleach, bleach can be used as a disinfectant. Or to treat water by using eight drops of regular household liquid bleach per gallon of water. Do not use scented, colorsafe, or bleaches with added cleaners.
- Fire extinguisher
- Matches in a waterproof container
- Feminine supplies and personal hygiene items
- Mess kits: pots, pans, etc.
- Toiletry kit: Bug spray, toothpaste, toothbrushes, deodorant, sunscreen
- Paper cups, plates and plastic utensils, paper towels
- Paper and pencil
- Books, games, puzzles or other activities for children
- First aid kit: Supplement a typical kit with:
  - First aid book
  - Essential personal medications
  - Ibuprofen, aspirin, acetaminophen
  - Band aids
  - Bandages. Think small and large wounds
  - Triple antibiotic ointment
  - Scissors
  - All purpose cold medicine
  - Tweezers
  - Cotton balls
  - Swabs
  - Thermometer
  - Sanitary napkins
  - Small & large splints
  - Safety pins
  - Needle and thread
  - Pocket knife
  - Flashlight w/ batteries
  - Lightweight blanket
  - Antibiotics, if you can get extra
  - Prescription medications, get extra
  - Potassium Iodide (in the event of radiation)

- Good shoes: Shoes that you can walk in for miles and miles. Work boots or hiking boots are best over tennis shoes. Invest now in a few good pair of shoes for the family.
- Good socks: CoolMax for summer and SmartWool for winter
- Extra clothing: layers are best
- Rain ponchos, one per person
- Hand warmers
- Pet crates
- Pet food
- Pet food dishes

Home Emergency Supplies:

Water:
- 5 gallon water jugs, cleaned and filled. Clean 1 time/year
- Bleach: Regular household chlorine bleach.
  Note: Do not use scented, colorsafe, or bleaches with added cleaners.
- Medicine dropper
- Disinfectant to clean surfaces: When diluted nine parts water to one part bleach
- Drinking water: Mix drops of bleach in water, depending on how cloudy the water is. If water is cloudy, add up to double the amount of bleach. Stir or shake and let sit for 30 minutes.
  - 2 drops per quart
  - 8 drops of regular household liquid bleach per gallon of water
  - ½ teaspoon per 5 gallons
Note: Date your bleach bottles. They lose their effectiveness after one year.
- Rain barrels

Tools/Supplies:
- Duct tape
- Twine
- Tools to chop wood: ax, shovel, hoe, etc.
- Hand tools
- Manual can opener
- Extra sleeping bags for extra people
- Extra pillows, sheets, blankets, towels

Transportation:
- Bicycles
- Lock for each bike
- Moped
- Old cars (pre 1972) in event of an electromagnetic pulse

Cooking Alternatives:
A way to cook and heat water if electric goes out
- Grill
- Fire pit
- Wood stove
- Dutch oven
- Camp stoves
- Solar ovens (purchased from food storage companies)
- Volcano Collapsible Propane Grill (ZebGear.com)

Fuel:
- Wood: chopped, dried, ready for winter
- Extra tanks of propane, always filled or keep home tank filled
- Lots of charcoal briquettes (easier to store than wood)

- Kerosene
- Butane
- Newspaper logs: Roll newspapers from one corner to the other, tucking in the ends and secure the bundle with wire. Soak in water, so it shrinks up. Then, dry it out. Compact to stack easily and burns cleanly.
- Generator, if possible, only a good solution for short term outages
- XL extension cords to reach generator. Surge strips.
- Extra gasoline (rotate every 3-6 months)
- Cast iron pots
- Frying pans, dutch oven, etc.
- Heavy duty aluminum foil
- Cooking utensils
- Hot pads

Equipment for Cutting Wood:
- Chain saw
- Extra spark plugs, and spare chains
- Engine starting fluid
- Gasoline (8-10 gallons)
- 2 cycle oil (4 quarts)
- Oil and fuel mixing can
- Measuring cup
- Bar chain oil (2 quarts)
- Axes
- Bow saw
- Heavy leather gloves
- Safety goggles

Heat Source for House in Winter:
Check source of heat for winter now
- Does your fireplace heat the room?
- Do you need to prepare it to do so?
- Wood stove
- Generators usually can help you heat your house

Cooling in Summer:
- House fans in case air conditioning goes out

Communication:
Family Emergency Plan Items:
- Have a family meeting
- Plan as if you can't use cell phones, computers, GPS
- Print everyone's phone numbers and put in cars, wallets
- Print evacuation routes and store maps in cars, etc.
- Cell phones
- Cell chargers
- Walkie Talkies with lots of batteries
- Solar powered battery charger and rechargeable batteries
- Ham radios
- Crank (non battery) weather & emergency radio

Light Sources:
- Battery-powered spotlight
- Lanterns for main rooms. Extra wicks. Buy lots of oil now. (You can only find large jugs of oil at the hardware store but NOT Lowes, Home Depot, or Walmart unless it's in season).
- Several large boxes of matches. (Get at hardware store)
- Lighters
- Crank flashlights (Non-battery from Target/Walmart)
- Headlamps (camping)
- Solar-powered outdoor lights for paths. (Bring inside at night)
- Extra flashlight bulbs
- Liquid paraffin or liquid candles last up to 100 hours

Clothing:
- Good shoes for walking. Good hiking or work boots.
- Extra tennis/running shoes: winter boots if needed
- Socks: CoolMax in summer/SmartWool in winter
- Layers
- Fleece and wool
- Extra hats, gloves, scarves
- Lightweight summer clothing
- Work pants with pockets
- Work gloves, extra pairs for workers cutting wood, etc.

Personal Items:
- Brush, comb
- Deodorant
- Lotion
- Sunglasses
- Prescription glasses (extra pair)
- Contact lenses (extras)
- Underwear
- Bras

Toiletries:
- Feminine products
- Shampoo, conditioner
- Shaving cream
- Razors
- Toothpaste, toothbrushes
- Towels
- Washcloths
- Sunblock: get highest protection/waterproof
- Baby food
- Baby supplies

Sanitation:
- Toilet paper (use phone books if you run out)
- Bleach
- Hot water source to wash dishes and sponge bath
- Hand sanitizer
- Hand soap
- Dish soap
- Laundry soap
- Disinfectants
- Rags
- Towels
- Clothesline or rack
- Clothespins
- Washboard
- Tub

Sample Emergency Sanitation Kit:
- 5 gallon bucket: You can get free buckets at Sam's Club Bakery.
- Plastic 5 gallon trash bags that fit in bucket
- Toilet seat lid (screw on type)
- Lime or sawdust for the smell
- If you can still use toilets but are limited on water, use gray water that you captured outside to flush. Put the 5 gallon buckets with lids in each bathroom. Flush only brown. Put all paper in buckets inside smaller grocery sized bags.

Food:
- Basic baking: fats, sugar, spices
- Large bag of salt (Salt is an essential to preserve meat if freezer goes out).
- Grains: Large bags of dried beans, rice, cereals, pasta, oatmeal, instant noodles. (Use and rotate this food every six months. Store in dry cool place).
- Protein: Commercial and home canned meats, textured vegetable protein, peanut butter, dehydrated eggs, dried dairy
- Fruits and vegetables: Canned or dehydrated fruits and vegetables. Check out local Amish and Mormon stores.
- Canned soups, dehydrated soups
- Sauces
- Fun foods: Dry drink mixes, canned drinks, desserts, boxed mixes, condiments, additional spices
- Instant coffee or French press
- Vitamins
- Extra medications

Non-Food Items for Kitchen:
- Aluminum foil: Regular and heavy duty
- Waterproof matches
- Napkins
- Paper cups
- Paper plates
- Paper towels
- Plastic utensils
- Re-sealable plastic bags
- Trash bags
- Cleaners
- Bleach
- Clothesline and clothespins
- Dish soap
- Laundry soap
- Vinegar
- Large baking soda
- Anti-bacterial soap

Water Purification:
Pure clean water may become the #1 commodity
- Get some sort of family-sized water purifier with extra filters. Think about helping the neighbors who don't have good drinking water. www.Sawyer.com
- Rain barrels to capture rain water
- 5 Gallon Water bottles filled and stored in cool dry place
- Carry with you Katadyn water purification tablets

Note: PRACTICE using all your equipment before emergencies. Make it fun for the family when there's no stress.

My Additional Items: _____
_____
_____
_____
_____
_____

Justin & Kynada Boland
Bolands.ThriveLife.com **Shop**
816-853-0697 **Phone**

Cansolidator Pantry
HEIGHT **10.5"**   WIDTH **Varies**
DEPTH **16.5"**   CAN CAPACITY **40**

Cansolidator Cupboard
HEIGHT **9.5"**   WIDTH **Varies**
DEPTH **10.25"**   CAN CAPACITY **20**

Harvest 72"
HEIGHT **72"** WIDTH **36.5"**
DEPTH **24.5"**
CAN CAPACITY **460**

Harvest 72" #10
HEIGHT **72"** WIDTH **36.5"**
DEPTH **24.5"**
CAN CAPACITY **112**
#10/gallon-size cans

4 Side Shelves
WIDTH **18.5"**   DEPTH **24.5"**
WEIGHT CAPACITY **100 lbs/ea**

Top Shelf
WIDTH **36"**   DEPTH **24"**
WEIGHT CAPACITY **125 lbs**

Ready Rack
HEIGHT **72"**   WIDTH **36.5"**
DEPTH **24.5"**   CAPACITY **304**

2 PERSON SURVIVAL PACK
Equipped with the life-essential
gear 2 people need for 72 hours.

Top Seller 6 Pack

Instant Milk, Whole Egg Powder, Strawberries (FD), Hard White Winter Wheat, White Flour, and Quick Oats.

FD Meat 6 Pack

Sausage Crumbles (FD), Ground Beef (FD), Chicken Dices (FD) (2), Ham (FD), and Roast Beef (FD).

Mixed Veggie 6 Pack

Cauliflower (FD), Green Beans (FD), Chopped Onions (FD), Potato Chunks, Carrot Dices, and Sweet Corn (FD).

Dehydrated Fruit 6 Pack

Apple Slices, Apple Chips (2), Banana Chips (2), and Pineapple.

Mixed Berry 6 Pack

Blackberries (FD), Raspberries (FD) (2), Strawberries (FD) (2), and Blueberries (FD).

Island Fruit 6 Pack

Mandarin Oranges (FD), Mangoes (FD) (2), Banana Slices (FD)(2), and Pineapple (FD).

Green Veggie 6 Pack

Green Beans (FD), Green Peas (FD) (2), Chopped Spinach (FD) (1), Broccoli (FD), and Celery (FD).

Kids 6 Pack

Strawberries (FD), Elbow Macaroni (2), Mac & Cheese Sauce (2), and Non-fat Powdered Milk.

Entrée 6 Pack

Dijion Rice with Chicken, Mesquite BBQ Chicken, Chicken Curry, Sweet Pepper Steak, Chili and Vegetable Risotto.

Entrée Soup 6 Pack

Baked Potato Cheese Soup (2), Broccoli Cheese Soup (2), and Chicken Noodle Soup (2).

pantry-size cans

Fruit Sample Pack

Apple Slices, Banana Slices (FD), Blackberries (FD), Blueberries (FD), Mangoes (FD), Peach Slices (FD), Pineapple (FD), Raspberries (FD), and Strawberries (FD).

pantry-size cans

Veggie Sample Pack

Broccoli (FD), Cauliflower (FD), Celery (FD), Corn-Sweet (FD), Mushroom Pieces (FD), Chopped Onions (FD), Peas-Green (FD), Potato Chunks vand Green Bean (FD).

THRIVE
LIFE

Justin & Kynada Boland
Bolands.ThriveLife.com **Shop**
816-853-0697 **Phone**